HIERARCH COUNSELLING, (

ALEX H PARKER

Introduction

We are presented with Maslow's original 'five stage' Hierarchy of Needs in most courses on the subject of psychotherapy and care. It is generally believed that it assists the student to understand the principles behind human motivation and well-being. The subject is very deep and involves many principles determining the outcome of an individual's development and sense of fulfilment and self-esteem. There have been many attempts to improve or alter the original concept but it appears to offer the most concise and easy to follow description of human needs available to date. The hierarchy of needs is used to increase understanding of human development, human needs and human motivation. This book will also discuss the innate resources we possess to attain these needs and the blocks which frustrate development. We will concentrate on the core principles of 'Person Centred Philosophy' which will be presented as a 'value of personal character' rather than a professionally introjected reductive model. This is important because we cannot help another individual to attain self actualisation if we value professional development above personal development; we must have as part of our nature certain principles that are not motivated by dogmatic learning but rather through the wisdom of self knowledge. The Hierarchy of Needs was originally presented by Psychologist Abraham Maslow. It is a concept that originates from 'humanistic psychology' which has both Abraham Maslow and Carl Rogers attributed as its founders. They were both influential in the development of the human potential movement during the 1960's and their combined theories of humanistic psychology have transformed the fields of psychotherapy, teaching and social care, influencing governmental social policy throughout the developed world. From the inception of the hierarchy of needs and the development of the person centred approach the secular world has changed from an authoritarian society of 'one size fits all values,' to a liberal culture of acceptance and tolerance where the autonomy of the individual is valued. Both Maslow and Rogers developed their theories by making reference to psychological research and applying it to their work. Rogers expresses his enthusiasm for a scientific approach for validating his theories when he said on page 25 of Becoming a Person:

The Facts are always friendly. Every bit of evidence one can acquire, in any area, leads one that much closer to what is true.' (Rogers 1961)

Carl Rogers worked with juveniles in his early career and observed the effect that emotional deprivation has upon a child's development. His form of psychotherapy has been developed into an effective model for social work and teaching. Carl Rogers was able to present the subject of love in a scientifically credible way; he was able to present it from a point of view that would satisfy even the most dogmatic of empiricists. He explains on page 281 of the Carl Rogers Reader. *'I have been one of those who, over the past several decades, have pointed out the need for new models of science more appropriate to human beings.'* (Rogers 1989)

Love has always been the subject of poetry and philosophy. It has been represented scientifically as an 'attachment' with a 'view to survival' and the 'instinctive need to procreate,' Something as abstract as love is rather unquantifiable from a research point of view, but Carl Rogers was able to present the subject in a unique terms that answered many questions regarding 'what makes an individual happy and successful, or suffer from feelings of low self-worth?' His view on the subject correlates directly

4

with the social aspect of the hierarchy of needs, which is essential to fulfil if we are ever to reach the goal of self actualisation. There have been many effective forms of therapy based on a more 'logical positivist' perspective of human functioning which almost reduce humans to machines, but the therapy developed from humanistic psychology keeps the human complete, valuable. Rogers view recognises the importance of transcending our basic innate drives so that we can become more than the sum of our parts. 'Becoming all we can be' sounds an almost 'sage like' statement but it is one that describes Self actualisation quite well. Self-Actualisation is a form of transcendence but not in the spiritual sense, although many individuals say they have had moments of Self-Actualisation, this is probably been a state of euphoria which is massively and embarrassingly different to Self-Actualisation. Self-Actualisation is true autonomy with complete self determination and responsibility. This state is at the top of the hierarchy of needs because it has the other needs fulfilled as a prerequisite of its development. This includes the development of self-esteem and confidence. It will also include the freedom to think in unique, abstract and maverick ways without social inhibition. An individual who is self-actualised will be motivated by their enthusiasm to fulfil goals. If they want to do art they will do so. If they have a great idea they will follow it through. People who are self actualisers are comfortable with themselves and do not require the acceptance of others to feel valuable. They are not the kind of people who will follow the crowd or be content to accept principles that they feel are wrong. They are assertive in the sense that they have self-respect at the same time as respecting the rights of others. It is a matter of growth. A flower will actualise by blossoming and producing fruit or a coal miner you will create innovative ways to produce coal, a pilot will become an astronaut and a mother becomes the prime minister of Britain. Self-actualisation is the 'full realisation of one's potential' and is 'Growth motivated, instead of deficiency motivated'. Being growth motivated means to constantly have the drive to come to fruition. We could probably suggest a great many characteristics regarding the self actualised individual but we need to be careful not to turn the subject into some sort of pop psychology non sense. The self-actualised individual is motivated to fulfil their potential and because they already have self-esteem and self-acceptance, they do not need to compare themselves to others to maintain motivation and self-worth. These characteristics are skimmed over in many courses and especially in care. You will find that most Courses for care in the community wheel out the Hierarchy of Needs like a sacred scripture and offer a very shallow review of its principles making it extremely difficult for the student to understand its therapeutic application for the wellbeing and development of service users. The world of care has a history of regimented routines with punishments for patients and service users who do not conform to the system. This always meant that the system ran smoothly but service users would suffer. They would suffer because they were not classified as people but rather they were a problem that was being minimised through segregation and control. This sounds like a bleak view of the past attitude of care but this was a situation that was based primarily on compassion in a world that was dominated by religion and authoritarianism. Over the past thirty years the secular based 'Person Centred' values have been very slowly introduced into government legislation regarding the care and support of individuals. The education regarding those principles sometimes forgets its humanistic psychology basis and risks turning the philosophy into nothing more than a professional 'paper pushing' requirement. In order for Care staff to work according to a humanistic/person centred philosophy they need to first experience rigorous personal development to identify and eliminate any aspects of personality that may suppress a service users personal growth. They need to be able to identify and understand their reactions to some service users and avoid the natural tendency for prejudice and favoritism. Our own motivation to become a counsellor teacher or care worker may be the result of 'introjection' or our own need to be accepted or dominate others in some way or perhaps we want to have our ego tickled in some way. Many of the practitioners who enter into these professions have a need to become a rescuer or 'nurturing parent.' According to Transactional Analysis we have a tendency to display one of three ego states:

The Child Ego: Primarily concerned with automatic emotion, dependency, curiosity and play. Feelings and behaviour are produced by the child ego; these are either natural or adapted, depending on the social conditions being influenced primarily by significant adults. Subdivisions of the child ego are: Adapted child and Natural child.

Adult Ego: An objective state that can experience thoughts and emotions without allowing the emotion or thoughts to take away objectivity. The 'genuine self'. A mature and healthy individual with be primarily guided by their adult ego.

The Parent Ego: Mentally recorded values and behaviours from significant adults in our life. This can include nurturing qualities and authoritarian critical qualities. Subdivisions of the Parent ego are: Nurturing parent (giving care) or Critical Parent (chastisement and judgement).

The reason that many people in the Teaching, care and psychotherapy professions need to obtain rigorous personal development is their tendency to be motivated by their 'Parent Ego.' The Parent Ego is where all of the introjections are stored. These are the recordings we have stored from significant adults as we have grown up. These recordings can be critical and in psychotherapy we are often dealing with the recordings that have been assimilated into the critical side of the parent ego that we not only adopt but also act as an <u>internal critic</u> that guides our actions and feelings. Our significant adults also show us love; this is recorded as the nurturing side of the Parent Ego. For example; we record how it feels to be hugged and cared for when we are injured or when we are supported by words that validate our self-worth. People who have developed a strong Parent Ego can appear compassionate and empathic but this is not necessarily a representation of truth. The Parent Ego is a recording of significant adults who cared for us as a child. The love and caring we received as a child was valuable as we learnt what it feels like to be comforted and encouraged to develop. The difficulty is that as a fully grown adult you must adopt a Child Ego state to benefit from the nurturing effects of the Parent Ego from another individual. The Child Ego is seen in adults as much as it is seen in children. It can be witnessed in people who are feeling playful, flirtatious and when they are demonstrating curiosity; it is also observable in people who are feeling helpless. The Most passive or non-assertive people you will meet are usually in an Adapted Child state. They have learnt that defending yourself or being assertive results in punishment from a significant adult (in Critical Parent Ego) or that by behaving helplessly hooks the Nurturing Parent in others and as a result they will have things done for them. For example: Tommy had an unspecified disability and managed to get the social services to supply a housekeeping service, bathing service, day centre provision and a wheelchair that he didn't need. Eventually after several years it was discovered that he obtained these services by doing nothing more than claiming that he suffered from pains in the back and declaring in a sad voice that he was housebound. His wife had suffered from heart troubles before she died and he originally obtained social services assistance in caring for her. After her death Tommy realised that all the welfare benefits he was receiving would be taken away and so he overly emphasised his back pain in order to maintain his income. In effect Tommy had been conditioned to behave in a passive and helpless (Child Ego) way by care services that were dominated by people who have the tendency to have their Nurturing Parent hooked by such an individual. In effect the care services had disempowered this gentleman in their desire to fulfil their role as a Nurturing Parent. Care workers services are often manipulated by such individuals because their Nurturing Parent is normally always their executive ego state. The counselling profession is equally as likely to attract people who have a strong desire to express their Nurturing Parent but quite often student counsellors have the addition of an Adapted Child that they must overcome before they can practice therapy. Oddly enough, when they leave their training, neither the Parent nor the Child ego should be executive but rather the Adult Ego which is the objective self. The counselling profession attracts damaged people as its workforce. It is very difficult to find a counsellor who didn't enter into their training with a bag of issues that needed to be addressed before they could ever hope to offer a professional service. The process of identifying our own issues are:

- To identify deficiencies in their own personal growth that may limit their effectiveness within the professional relationship.

- To have an avenue for dealing with personal issues so that these do not intrude into the professional relationship.

A client can expect to enter into counselling and find they are in the presence of an individual who has put their own issues to rest and can listen to the client with empathy. When the client talks about their angry father, the counsellor doesn't immediately become distracted by thoughts about their own angry father and feel compelled to talk about it or offer advice. If a client experiences transference and states that they view the therapist as a grandfather figure, then by means of personal development a therapist can identify this and prevent a mutual response. A mutual response where the therapist accepts the imposed role is known as contertransference. This is a phenomenon is experienced by the therapist toward the client. It can include falling in love or accepting an inappropriate role. A tendency to take on this grandparent role would alter the relationship from an objective Adult Ego into a Nurturing

Parent to Adapted Child role; in effect the therapist has allowed the Child Ego to hook his Nurturing Parent. It causes us to go into our own frame of reference and confuse the clients experience as similar to our own and as a result we are no longer trying to understand the client and are becoming a nurturing parent who is judging the client albeit positively. Being effected by the client's issues is a danger that many counsellors discover early in their training. There can become a compulsion to Judge the clients experience and motivations based on your own experiences. When this is the case you could begin talking as if you have a great insight based on your subjective experience, which will distract from the clients unique situation and destroy the therapeutic relationship. Rogers (1980) States:

"This is true because it is impossible to accurately perceive another's inner world if you have formed an evaluative opinion of that person. "
A way of Being (1980) page 154

In these circumstances the professional imposes themselves on the client through the belief that they know exactly what the client is feeling or thinking. There are times when a counsellor enters into a relationship with a client and it becomes apparent that the counsellor is experiencing a reaction to the client's story. Perhaps the counsellor experiences more anger than could be explained by empathy, perhaps the counsellor can't help thinking about the clients circumstances because in some way they are too familiar to their own. Most counsellors find that this can be alleviated if they have continuous therapy and supervision. Not all issues can be ironed out in five years of training. The main thing that a counsellor needs to accomplish is to gain Awareness of their ego states. Frederick Perls et al (1951) states:

"The basic endeavour is to assist you to become aware of how you are functioning as an organism and as a person. Since you are the only one who can make the necessary observations, we shall... be dealing with "private events."
Gestalt Therapy Frederik Perls et al , (1951)

Once we become conscious of our ego states we are then able to address the issues that they present us with. Entering into counselling training the trainee may have been driven by their Parent Ego to become something virtuous and caring to placate the internal needs created by their own Parent Ego. We may have craved acceptance as a child which was never fulfilled unless you conformed to your parent's values. If you are able to become that parent that you introjected then perhaps you gain a sense of self-worth. Many people go through life trying to please their parents even after those parents have died. They still exist in our mind and we can hear/feel their voice of praise and criticism for the actions we take as an adult. Some people will be strongly motivated by those voices as they evoke feelings of guilt and anxiety if disobeyed. Others will experience those thoughts and continue on their own path with no feelings of guilt. It is interesting that the trainee counsellor will normally enter into training to make use of their parent ego but on beginning to receive counselling in the classroom they retire into their child ego state and find that they are bombarded by emotions and issues that they had suppressed for many years. The child ego state is a very powerful state to evoke. Many of us will do anything to keep it suppressed and avoid the emotions that it brings. James & Jongeward (1971) state:

When people are badly hurt, their natural child wants to scream, cry and demand care. Their Adapted Child may withdraw in silent agony, especially if they learned in childhood that crying brought spanking.
Born to Win by James & Jongeward. 1971.

Ego states are like fishermen who are constantly trying to cast out their line and hook a fish. The parent ego attempts to hook the child ego in another person. If I behave in nurturing parent when I am with Jim then I am trying to hook his natural child. If I am angry and in critical parent with Jim then I am trying to get him to hook his adapted child and make him submit to my authority. Many people are susceptible to having their 'adapted child' hooked by the authoritarian behaviour of another. People who are susceptible to becoming passive and docile when presented with someone who is expressing their 'critical parent' are in effect submitting to the others dominance. It is an interesting dynamic to watch. If you watch two people arguing aggressively they are both in 'critical parent' and fighting to hook their opponents 'adapted child'. They will raise their voices higher and higher, perhaps they will get to the point of bad language and physical violence. The scenario is a game where one of the arguing parties will retire into adapted child mode and either become passive or begin to cry. This is a very unhealthy relationship and is more akin to the fight for dominance in the wild rather than something we would recognise as human, and yet being aware of a tendency to behave this way is very rare. When working with people in care it is common to see the professional adopting a nurturing parent role, unfortunately when they encounter challenging behaviour from a service user they may adopt a critical parent role. This type of transaction is a recipe for disaster. Whether it is working with older people or with people who experience learning disabilities it is important to remember that they are paying for a service and it is our responsibility to help them foster autonomy and authority in their own life. We need to address our service users' needs without humiliating them. Strengthening the Adult Ego assists the professional to perceive the situation objectively. In certain situations a care professional may be dealing with a service user who is uncooperative and as a result experience feel frustration. The natural reaction to frustration is anger. This is because the body produces the right amount of hormones to deal with irritation. In the unenlightened days of the past teachers and care professionals were permitted to administer physical punishments to accompany their frustration and address challenging behaviour. It was common place to find a school would use the cane to hit a child across the bottom or use a wooden ruler to hit the child across the hand. Frustration is a natural emotion to experience but it will not be dealt with professionally unless the individual has a dominant Adult ego. The Adult ego is a state of mindfulness. It is able to experience events and emotions objectively and examine them without being dominated by them. The adult ego is also a position of logical evaluation rather than emotionally based judgements. The beauty of the adult ego is that it opens the door to equal communication. This doesn't mean that a professional will walk around like a robot but rather there the professional with a dominant 'Adult ego' will be able to experience the 'child ego' and 'parent ego' states in a regulated way rather than through conditioning or instinctive reflex. Person centred/ humanistic principles require that our service users and clients be able to grow in their own unique way rather than being for forced to conform to a service or a professionals requirements. The parent ego therefore is a position of power over others whether it is nurturing or critical and this is why a teacher, psychotherapist and care worker needs to be aware of the ego state they allow to be executive in their interactions. It is a requirement of anyone studying counselling and psychotherapy that they receive rigorous therapy themselves in order to identify any incongruities and areas for personal development that need to be addressed before being let loose on the public. Problems that can sabotage the professional relationship; such as transference, counter transference, projection and unconscious prejudice and authoritarian attitudes are all caught in the net and dealt with when personal development and supervision are taken seriously. For the Counsellor and psychotherapist Personal Development enables the trainee to accept the client unconditionally. This cannot always be said for care. In the UK there has been a drive to assist care workers to be more professional. People who work in care are generally a level 2 (GCSE) standard or level 3 (A level) for supervisors at the highest, with some requirement for rigorous personal development. The supervision they receive is often delivered by trainers who may not have been trained in the principles of supervision but it is enough to cover auditing requirements and is generally a mere shadow of its true purpose. This is to be expected. In a world with an ageing population the need to have care services is essential and training staff is a time consuming endeavour which presents an almost impossible task for the cash strapped employer. This is worrying because without vigorous personal development some care workers are unable to differentiate between their own aggression and assertiveness or understand that encouraging obedience and cooperation are two different approaches that require very different attitudes. In this type of environment there can be no hope of encouraging Self Actualisation if the workers own growth is stunted by a lack of personal development. Some healthcare workers chose the job because they need to express their 'nurturing parent' in order to feel and sense of self-worth; but to pursue their own self-worth as 'Nurturing Parent' for their own gratification requires the service user to surrender their autonomy and independence and would be counterproductive to the therapeutic environment. This is often a difficult problem to detect as it is very easy for someone to take on the role of dependant if nobody is overlooking the situation: Mr Jones suffered a slight learning disability but it was so mild that no one really noticed. He attended a day centre three days a week where he enjoyed playing pool with friends. Betty was a 'senior care worker' from the day centre and took a particular shine to Mr Jones because he reminded her of her late granddad who required round the clock care. Mr Jones was living independently and only needed assistance to fill in forms and to be advised to go to the doctors if he was poorly, apart from that he was able to function adequately. On one of his annual medical check-ups it was discovered that he had high blood pressure and as a result he was prescribed medication to lower it which caused him to feel faint in the first few weeks until the doctor got the dosage correct. Betty immediately made preparations to assist him cope with his new disability. She used her influence and arranged 'meals on wheels' to be delivered to his home. She used her seniority to arrange for another care worker to give him a bath at the day centre twice a week. Mr Jones became increasingly anxious because of the extra help and began to think he was more disabled that he actually was. He was encouraged to stay within the confines of the day centre and to have someone carry his food to his table. This was a serious situation because Mr Jones who was quite independent beforehand was now being scared into obeying baseless authoritarian recommendations from Betty that always included 'Nurturing Parental' phrases "we'll do this because we wouldn't want anything to happen to you." This gentleman was terrified. He stayed in his home and stopped his usual shopping activities. Because he didn't understand the reason that he was being bathed at the day centre he completely neglected his personal hygiene at home. Because he didn't understand the reason that care workers were carrying his food to the table at the day centre he assumed his condition required him to avoid such tasks altogether and asked the meals on wheels delivery man to bring his carton of food into his house and place it on the table. Eventually Mr Jones became dishevelled and depressed. He was in constant need of reassurance and would ask Betty's permission before making any decision. Mr Joneses 'Adapted Child' had been hooked by the well meaning intentions of Betty's 'Nurturing Parent.' At least that is a kind way to put it. Betty's actions were actually abuse. She was in effect taking a healthy independent man and taking away his confidence and autonomy. She was making him dependant on her in order to feed her desire to be a 'nurturing parent.' If Mr Jones were to break any of the rules she had created she would become slightly angry and tell him to let someone else do the task. In this way her 'critical parent', became active until he retired to his 'adapted child' and submitted to Betty's conditions. It was easy for Betty to use her position to disempower a service user, for three reasons:

- She claimed her actions were compassionate and anyone who disagreed was abandoning Mr Jones.
- She claimed to know the details of Mr Jones condition.
- Other staff were not prepared to challenge her decision.

This situation highlights the how easy it is to work in opposition to a person centred/ humanistic philosophy while at the same time maintain a façade of care. Mr Jones's quality of life and mental health were badly damaged by the selfish actions of Betty who could only find self-worth by rendering another individual dependant upon her. Of course Betty was not conscious that she was abusing Mr Jones, but this is why there is a need for continuous personal development for those who desire to enter into the helping professions. Betty held a self-concept that told her that she was caring and compassionate when in fact she was acting like an opportunist parasite who was in effect feeding her ego from Mr Jones's misfortune. Betty was able to get away with were treatment of Mr Jones because there is general confusion regarding the principles of a Person Centred/

Humanistic philosophy. Local government in the UK have often taken advantage of this ignorance and perverted the principles of a person centred philosophy to justify the closure of care homes and respite day care. This action always results in social loss, depression and death of a great number of service users. They have accomplished this by re-framing the act of 'abandonment to save cash' into a disingenuous intention of 'promoting independence'. Generally speaking, the care industry has adopted Person Centred/Humanistic values and is continuously improving its employees needs but it will take time before the care industry begins to apply the person centred philosophy beyond a paper pushing exercise that only exist to please auditors, but there are examples of individual care workers who not only understand a person centred/ humanistic approach but also enhance its effects through their commitment to providing the ideal conditions for growth. Commitment to the advancement of service users or clients requires that their contracted 'service providers' supply an environment that stimulates growth. For flowers; sunlight fertile soil and water are needed for optimum growth and if these elements are in balance the flower will flourish and produce fruit or a gorgeous display of colour. Humans also require a fertile and balanced environment to flourish. This environment is usually provided in the family home but can also be found in school or in the therapy room or anywhere else that a healthy relationship can be developed with other people. There is no such thing as a self-made individual; we all rest on the shoulders of those who contributed to the perfection of our environment. Our perfect environment requires the efficient provision of:

Each of these needs is placed in order of priority and the mind of the individual will focus on fulfilling each need in succession perhaps to the point of obsession, we will discuss how this is expressed in detail later. Self actualisation is not a guarantee for all people. To have self-esteem is the gift of a supportive social environment and results in a happy confident outlook. Perhaps the environment does not provide all the resources required for self actualisation to be expressed fully in the individuals own unique way, but certainly the individual can find satisfaction. Self-esteem is a wonderful quality that people would benefit from developing. To feel comfortable and confident in your abilities and to be comfortable and satisfied regarding your inadequacies is a peaceful place to be. Being in such a frame of mind provides the individual with self-awareness and self-acceptance. People who have their esteem needs fulfilled are able to express the same value of acceptance to other people. How self-esteem is developed is not always based on a healthy experience of social fulfilment. Esteem may develop as a result of obeying rules and conditions which have been adopted from significant adults as a child, and result a very conditional form of self-esteem develops which will disintegrate into self-loathing and condemnation if those introjected ideals are not followed closely. The environment supplies the resources that contribute to the fulfilment of the hierarchy of needs. Whether working in Psychotherapy, Care or Teaching the aim should be to provide an environment where esteem can flourish.

Development in the Social Environment.

The environment is a resource for growth. As a child we are helpless and are dependant on the good will of other humans to provide our basic needs. If we are not accepted by our parents it is unlikely that we will survive for long as we would soon starve from neglect. Social workers see the results of neglected children on a regular basis. Whether it is a result of substance abuse or mental health issues of the parent, the needs of severely neglected children are rarely fulfilled even to the most basic level. James was born to a mother who desperately wanted a baby. His mother kept her own family at a distance because she felt their offers of support implied that she was not a capable mother. No one really knew how James was cared for in his early years but it was clear when the social workers arrived that it was with the minimal intervention from his mother. He was five years old by this time. He couldn't talk and still wore nappies which were discarded around the home with an abundance of wine bottles at the foot of the settee and his mother's bed. He learned to survive by drinking water from the tap or toilet. He appeared to live on convenience foods or biscuits or anything that needs no preparation. His basic needs were fulfilled by adapting to his environment by independently find resources for his survival. For such a neglected child the parent is absent or represents a minimum resource for care. Safety needs are compromised because there is no way of predicting the future, no routine, no security, stability or regular meal times. James received the minimum amount of communication from his mum while he was in her care and as a result he didn't develop discernible speech and he struggled at school with underdeveloped learning and social skills. The environment that James was living in was minimising his ability to develop. Certainly, he survived because the innate human resources acted as his drive to help him attain the basic needs of food and water but as for the higher needs he could not hope to thrive unless he was removed and placed into an environment that was able to supply the resources that helped him to develop.

James was placed into a foster home with three other children who encouraged him to play. Although he did display some challenging behaviour he was rewarded for every step of development he made and rapidly began to make progress in speech and social skills. His foster parents were patient with him and offered him unconditional love. The result was that by the time he was ten years old that he was able to maintain relationships and pursue some interests in clay modelling and scouts. James had experienced the extreme of deprivation where his basic needs where fulfilled by his adaptive behaviour but his higher needs safety and social needs were only fulfilled when his environment became supportive of his growth. It could be argued that the most important and influential aspect of the hierarchy is the Social Needs because this stage is like a cross roads that can lead to Self Actualisation or the stunted neurotic generating 'Actualising of an ideal.' Actualising an ideal is very different from self actualisation and is the reason many people come for therapy. The 'ideal' that is discussed is one that does not belong to the individual but is rather imposed upon them during the social stage as a requirement for receiving love and acceptance. For humans the social needs are apparent throughout the basic needs and safety needs. Certainly we will use this experience to measure our value based on how these needs have been fulfilled, which will contribute toward fulfilling subsequent esteem needs; however the child will not fixate on these the social needs if the need to rummage for food dominates their drive for survival. On page 115 of the Carl Rogers Reader he states:

"One of the many interesting and challenging implications of this study, one seems reasonably clear. It is that no amount of direct food reward can take the place of certain perceived qualities, which the infant appears to need and desire."

The family are the strongest influence upon an individual's development and may offer acceptance and love if the child behaves in accordance to specific rules. The story of 'the neglect of James' was one we may never encounter but most people can relate to the 'social requirement to conform.' This can result in an adult who has been conditioned from childhood to think in a certain way. Perhaps the son will be persuaded to classify his desire to be a musician as 'a foolish dream' and instead follow his father's advice and become a coal miner. Perhaps the daughter will marry someone from the same religion and live as a subservient wife to make the family proud. Whatever the condition placed upon an individual it will have serious effects upon the direction the individual's life takes. The rules for gaining love or acceptance are called 'conditions of worth' and they exist in most social situations but will be most dominant when 'introjected' or assimilated into the psyche as a child. A little girl may want to play football with the boys in the street but is discouraged from doing so by traditionalist parents who tell her that 'It is a game for boys' and that little girls should find less aggressive activities to get involved in. One day the father sees his daughter playing in the street with the football and comes running out of the house waving and shouting. He fears that his delicate daughter will be hurt in this aggressive game and wants to protect her, but instead of communicating his anxiety he instead expresses his anger. He shouts at her in the street and takes her into the house and shouts again. He then withdraws affection from his daughter to emphasise his annoyance. She is frightened by this experience her social and safety needs are threatened. To repair and maintain her father's affection she adopts or 'introjects' his 'conditions of worth.' Perhaps an example that most people can relate to is a religious one: Bartholomew was brought up as a Jehovah's Witness but the story could easily have been any religion that imposes dogmatic values. He was taught that anything outside the church is to be viewed with suspicion and any values outside the church are Satanic. He was conditioned to pray before each meal and to study the Bible regularly. In those days he was required to attend the Religious meetings and study groups three times a week and to take part in preaching activities as often as possible. He was told that to 'allow yourself to look at a woman and be attracted to her' is perverted and that he should pray for strength if he felt sexually weak. He was warned about the evil of masturbation and warned to have little association with those outside the church. His family and other congregation members were the only people he would socialise with. If he was to have his social needs fulfilled he would need to introject these conditions of worth or risk being expelled from the congregation where even his own family would reduce contact with him. This was a serious threat not only to his social needs but also to his 'safety needs' as the predictability that obedience brings also supplied protection in so many ways. In effect he was threatened with abandonment and neglect. From an early age, Bartholomew began to actualise an ideal. He followed the rules dogmatically and reported fellow members of the church to the elders if he suspected them of wrong doing and rewarded other members with praise and privilege if they excelled in following the interjects of the church. He eventually became a church elder and was respected for giving good talks and encouraging people to do the work of preaching. His parents were proud and his friends admired him and others aspired to be like him. He had become all he could be within those 'conditions of worth.' He was not happy. He had secretly learnt to play the guitar as a child and would fantasise about being a rock star. He would secretly fantasise about women but pretend he was disgusted by their immodest dress. At school he socialised with friends and desired to meet them at night but he was too scared to do so in case he was discovered. He even fell in love with a girl at work who seemed very interested in pursuing a relationship and she would flirt with him at every opportunity, but he reduced contact with her to prevent temptation. To the congregation he was the image of success but he was unfulfilled. He had actualised an Ideal. The ideal was created by the church and he introjected those conditions in order to fulfil his social needs in the same way a dog learns to role on its back for a treat. Self actualisation would have been a very different experience as Daniel his older brother found out. Daniel decided to leave the church when he was fifteen years old. He fell in love with a girl from school and told his parents that he was having tea with her parents one Sunday after their religious meeting. The parents immediately phoned the elders of the church who came to the house to question him. He told them that he was in love. They then asked him if he had any sexual contact and he said 'only kissing.'

This was enough. The elders gave him an ultimatum: Either repent and end the relationship or face being disfellowshiped from the church. This was not a problem; he had already written his resignation letter and handed it to the shocked Elders. Daniels parents and siblings reduced their contact with him to the point of only speaking to tell him that his meals were ready. A few months later Daniel left school and found a job at the local sandwich shop and spent his nights at college and became very close to his girlfriend's family. Eventually he started his own business and married his sweetheart. How lovely. Daniel became a self-actualised individual, never doubting his self, always believing he was valuable and possessing the self-esteem to make plans to move forward without the approval of his closest family.

Both brothers actualised but it was the quality of that actualisation that made the difference. 'Actualising an ideal' didn't work for Bartholomew. He did get married, but to a woman who was attracted to him because her parents were impressed that he was a spiritual man and had position in the church. She cherished the position of being a 'minister's wife.' They lived together in peace but without love and both functioned to please their parent's ideals and to maintain their position in the religious community.

In this story it is the social environment that makes the difference between the two brothers. Bartholomew is like an apple tree that is grown in a restrictive pot and cannot produce much fruit because his nutrients are in a confined place and dependant on the gardener to water the soil. Daniel is like an apple tree that is in a restrictive pot that has cracked at its bottom. His roots have been able to exploit the crack and find rich soil outside the pot. As a result, he has flourished independently of the gardener, producing fruit from every branch. In effect Daniel found acceptance outside the family and church. He had found love and belonging within another family and this contributed to his sense of self-worth and contributed to his transcendence.

The environment is where we find our physical and emotional resources for personal growth. We learn to become independent and self-actualise or remain dependant on the conditions of others. I may risk labouring the point too strongly but it is an important one: How our social needs are met determines whether we self-actualise.

Being born with a severe disability will often mean that an individual will spend most of their life developing a relationship with one family carer and develop friends within a social care setting, such as day centre or club. For many years people with a lifelong disability were hidden away from the rest of society and as a result society generally did not accept them. Humanistic principles were introduced into care settings for people with learning disabilities throughout the developed world with a view to supplying their needs and stimulate self-esteem, but this has been a slow and little understood process. Health care organisations are encouraged to develop Person centred Support plans for service users where the service moulds itself to the individual needs of the service users rather than requiring the service user to mould themselves to the needs of the service. This is has been a very difficult task as many individuals over the past twenty years have been rehoused from confined prison like institutions to supported housing where support is available to assist them live independently. This has been a very effective move but it has also been a very difficult transition for a great many service users. Independence cannot be thrust upon people if they have been conditioned to be dependant. For example, many individuals were in care settings where meals were made for them and served at their table. This was convenient for staff who could serve a large number of people in a short time. 'Independent living' service users are supported to make their own meals which is both time consuming and requires risk assessment and potentially the supply of specific tools that will enable the service user to accomplish these tasks independently. This is important for their development as fulfilled human beings. It is easy to supply people with basic needs and safety needs in such a care setting but it is very difficult for services to provide social and esteem needs that support autonomy. It is much easier to create conditions of worth and condition a group of service users to follow a uniformed code of behaviour for convenience than it is to encourage independence. It was common to see buses filled with people who have learning disabilities on their way to attend the same activities together and to have their meals at a set time and also to access the toilet at prearranged regimented times. Now people are supported on a one to one basis to make goals and move toward their individual outcomes. These goals can be virtually anything within reason. Being able to climb mountains, take part in campaigns or find a job are all things that are achievable in a country that supports a person centred 'humanistic' philosophy.

In care it is vital that people are supported to function autonomously otherwise they will never find fulfilment. This is difficult for many reasons but one of the most fundamental reasons is fixation on the safety needs. Safety needs are fulfilled in a situation where everything is decided for us and we can predict or future with certainty. The security that comes from such a situation is addictive and also reduces stress for a great many individuals. To be asked to make a decision about your desires can be an extremely frightening task if you have never thought about such things before and if changes will accompany the decision then the ability to predict the future will be impossible. For many individuals this is too much and they will refrain from making a decision so someone else will take the responsibility. This is true for most humans; we crave the safety and stability of the status quo. When working with people in life coaching it is the realisation that the changes will find success that stops them progressing rather than the belief that they will fail. Failure is a relief for some who would embark on change.

The environment is key to supplying the resources to assist an individual to climb the steps of actualisation. The worst thing that a support worker can do is to make the principles of personal advancement a condition of worth. A great many workers go the opposite way and make the principles of humanistic psychology and introject the values as conditions of worth; imposing its values like scriptural dogma onto all the people they can preach to. Humanistic psychology needs to be applied with respect for where the individual is at that time of their life. We can only ever provide the environment to assist them to grow and be nurtured as the growth is something that will happen as a natural result of what is provided. To demand that someone grows is to impose our own belief system onto them which in effect takes away their autonomy. The actualising tendency is a drive that is evident in all of nature and will happen when conditions are favourable.

The Environment, Actualising Tendency and Transcendence.

All life appears to have an actualising tendency. This would make biological sense, because if life didn't continuously transcend its needs it could not make the advancements that it has. Biology tells us that the history of every animal on the planet originates from a one celled organism; how this organism came to be self-replicating is down to its perfect environment. This is an unusual event. It is estimated that the chances of this happening are next to impossible. And yet within a galaxy of one hundred billion stars and an estimated nine hundred billion planets it did happen to our lonely planet. It is estimated by astronomers that in our massive galaxy that it would be unlikely to find more than a handful of planets where cells have begun to self replicate and evolve into complex organisms; and yet this doesn't mean that they will all have intelligence. And yet on our planet this one celled organism divided and became many millions; slowly spreading across the earth and adapting to their environment through a process of natural selection, to become the many millions of species we see today. Humans have developed from hunter gatherers who would work together to hunt meat and find edible fruits and berries; and for some reason, ten thousand years ago we developed farming and created towns and trading. We became the masters of the earth and the beast and we benefited from our relationships with other communities. We were becoming something new and instead of being shaped by our environment we learned to shape our environment to fit our needs. Like a tree that never stops growing the human race transcended its needs and had the time to ponder philosophy and science; developing complex writing, mathematics, art, laws, and education. After only 6500 years the communities had created civilisations that had built the pyramids in Egypt. The human race has continue to develop in ways that serve their basic needs but also go beyond their needs as if there is some drive that compels them to accomplish apparently unnecessary things such as climbing Everest, reaching the South Pole and landing on the Moon. It is as if life has a need to become all they can be or as Abraham Maslow expressed it:

"What a man can be, he must be. This is what we call self actualisation."
Maslow, A. (1954). *Motivation and personality.* New York, NY: Harper. pp. 91.

Self actualisation is the ultimate expression of the Actualising Tendency. The actualising tendency is active throughout each stage of the hierarchy of needs, it is the drive that keeps living organisms alive by continuously looking for avenues and resources to grow. Carl Rogers likened the Actualising Tendency to a potato he witnessed that had sprouted within a basement. Like all potatoes it sprouted roots to find food and when unable to find sustenance it used its own resourced to sprout a shoot with a flimsy flower that weakly searched for sunlight from a small window. Despite its environments inadequacies the potato was driven to become all that it could be. If that potato had been planted in a garden with water and sunlight it would have produced beautiful flowers and many new potatoes that would feed a family and potentially contribute to a new crop of potatoes. In many ways people are like the potato that is dependant on its environment for growth. The difference between us and a potato is that the potato will grow and become healthy when transplanted to fertile soil but humans carry our environment within their mind and often fail to grow as a result of their conditioning from childhood.

The actualising tendency will still be felt in a state of unrest or discontent and feel the desire but feel disempowered by introjects or a truly restrictive environment. Not everyone will self-actualise even if conditions are favourable but the actualising tendency is always present and psychotherapists, care workers and teachers are trained to provide an environment that stimulates growth. The therapeutic environment is like a well watered garden with full sunlight. The gardener has removed a plant from a pot that has restricted the roots and prevented it from growing. He gently unravels the roots so they no longer grow in the shape of the pot and are able to grow into the soil and feed the plant. The therapist will provide an environment that assists an individual to identify their own restricted roots in the form of introjects and conditions of worth. These values are usually applied in person centred counselling but they have been transferred into care and teaching to encourage wellbeing and growth by supporting people who have needs that are complicated by conditioning to a restrictive environment.

The Conditions for Growth.

The Humanistic approach addresses the humans as a whole being. This includes much more than the mind and body but also their environment and also the objects and people that the individual might classify as contributing to their sense of self. Anything that is included in a concept of self is called an ego boundary. Perls States:

"One person and another, are confluent when there is no appreciation of a boundary between them, when there is no discrimination of the points of difference or otherness that distinguish them."
Gestalt therapy Frederick Perlse Et al. (1951). Page 118.

To really know an individual with their motivations and needs we must understand their whole concept of self including social roles and boundaries to self. A boundary to self can include anything that contributes to our sense of self and include children, parents, and friends. It can include our job, our title, our social class or anything else that is identified as an important part of self. For many people losing any aspect of their ego boundary through death, economic troubles or job loss can result in an identity crisis where the individual feels lack of purpose or meaning and can be as traumatic as losing a limb. A mother might identify her children as being part of her identity and this motivates her to keep them close to her and control their actions and beliefs. But when they get married and leave home the mother falls into a depression until she can reinvest her energies elsewhere. In the care setting many people include the institution as part of their ego boundary. This is especially true if the care setting fosters dependency on its service. One of the most misapplied principles of person centred approach I witnessed in a care setting was in a day centre that worked with people who experienced physical disabilities and rehabilitation issues. Instead of encouraging service users to outgrow the service they were instead encouraged to adopt a role within the service as committee members who would govern activities. The purpose of creating the committee was to promote autonomy of the committee members; the committee members would then represent the needs of other service users. In effect the committee members identified themselves with this role very quickly and the whole institution was enveloped by their ego boundary. The effect was disastrous for a day centre that hoped to develop a person centred philosophy. The committee members began dominating the day centre activities effectively turning it into a bingo hall for their own gratification. The committee members identified so closely with their own role that none of them made any progress toward rehabilitation and to secure the day centres archaic and institutional approach they discouraged other service users from making progress by offering advice on how to create fictitious medical symptoms to secure and increase their welfare benefits.

The service users who used their own cars were encouraged to leave them at home at receive government funded day centre buses to pick them up which meant they were dependant on the institution to take them home a specific time in the afternoon, in effect they had no means to leave the day centre until closing time. In this way the committee members were dependant on the institution and the other service users to maintain their social role. The effect was that an institution had been created within an institution in which no one found fulfilment outside their artificial setting and were confined to a building that required attendees to mould themselves to the service rather than encourage them to follow their own interests. By contrast I worked in a charity run mental health 'drop in centre.' The policies of the drop in centre were to 'support people in their move toward self actualisation.' They offered life coaching to people who wanted to improve their life and they were successful in helping people build the confidence to devise a plan and move toward their goals. The difference between the two services was their understanding of human needs and that the staff had received rigorous personal development. They were also committed to understanding the person centred philosophy and applied its principles in their own life instead of making it a misunderstood paper exercise. The principles of person centred approach were originally a psychotherapy based philosophy and when applied in a care setting the effect is that the care service becomes a therapeutic service. The word care implies dependency and helplessness whereas if the term therapeutic support was used instead the perception of a service would be changed. Many services that offer support to people with disabilities and have changed the name of their care plans to support plans to emphasise their commitment to the advancement of the service user. Effective support plans include goal setting and regular reviews to monitor progress and make adjustments. In effect many support services have become therapeutic and their care workers have become in effect life coaches.

Therapeutic Attitudes for Practice.

We will now discuss the conditions that the professional needs to adopt to stimulate the clients natural tendency for growth and fulfilment. Being able to understand these principles beyond a superficial glance helps the practitioner to assess their own personal development. It is sometimes a matter of pride that prevents us from accepting that we are not as mature as our ego likes to believe, but as already discussed it is very unlikely that an individual will choose to work in care, counselling or psychotherapy unless they have an overly executive 'Parent ego'.

The use of technique is the contributing factor in most therapies but 'Person Centred Approach' concentrates more on the personal qualities of the therapist as the primary ingredient in a client's increased sense of well-being. Rogers recommended that these qualities be extended from therapy to include any profession that works with people including teaching and care. These qualities are not to be presented as a professional façade that can be switched on and off; rather they are qualities that should be part of the individual's personality. Since we are very unlikely to be born with these characteristics it is likely that we need to develop them through some serious personal development. We will now examine these qualities.

When working to a humanistic/ Person centred Philosophy the therapist will have developed three qualities that work together to produce an effective approach. These qualities are: Congruence, empathy and unconditional positive regard.

Congruence:

Congruence is a state of agreement within oneself. Rogers used congruence synonymously with the word 'genuiness' to explain the relationship we hold with ourselves. It involves honest communication with others and with ourselves. This requires an executive 'Adult Ego.' This will be experienced in the moment and it can be lost when we deny aspects of our experience or are faced with competing values. We all experience our actual self and ideal-self may not be in harmony. The Ideal Self is similar to the ego ideal as described by Sigmund Freud which is how we believe we should be. When our experiences of 'self' conflicts with ideal-self then we feel anxiety and attempt to deny the experience from awareness. Some people carry an Ego Ideal of peace and love only to be taken by surprise when they are faced with feelings of anger and hate. Anger and hate are feelings that cannot be accepted into their self-concept and so they deny the unacceptable aspects of themselves and in effect reject their true self. A client who denies aspects of self is presenting a façade in which it takes energy to maintain. If you try to maintain a smile while thinking of the saddest event in your life then you will find the fake smile very difficult to maintain without a certain amount of fatigue and stress. A façade is any behaviour that prevents an individual from being genuine. When we work in a professional capacity there is a tendency for some to hide behind 'pretence' based on their own Ego Ideal. For the Counsellor or care worker this pretence would probably be based on the nurturing qualities of the Parent Ego. We can link incongruence to any aspect in our mind that causes conflict but nothing is more damaging to the professional relationship than a non-genuine approach. All professionals need to be aware of their tendency to be incongruent and where these conflicts might arise. I was aware of a fundamentalist Christian woman who worked as a receptionist in a maternity hospital who was faced with a dilemma. As she processed some documents she discovered that one of the women from her church had opted to have a termination due to sever medical problems. She was obliged to disclose this information to her church ministers according to her indoctrinated 'ego ideal' but her commitment to professional confidentiality conflicted with her decision making. The conflict caused great anxiety but she concluded that 'there is no authority except God' and reported the matter to her ministers. After the ministers contacted the patient to question her about the reported 'sin' it was obvious to her where the information had come from, and after an investigation by the hospital the receptionist lost her job. The receptionist had two conflicting ethical ideas and both could not be acted upon. Congruence/ genuiness are not something that we can put off investigating, we need to continuously use personal development courses and supervision to identify exactly how we can identify and put to rest incongruity. If we hold a prejudice against someone of a certain ethnic group are uncomfortable with homosexuals or condemn prochoice, then you will fail as a professional therapist and be ineffective support worker / Carer. The failure comes from the fact that you will be unable to accept the person unconditionally. In other words we will maintain a façade or pretence of acceptance but will be spending energy in hiding our uncomfortable feelings and thoughts. Some student counsellors find that they cannot maintain the façade and resort to advice giving or try to lead the client into a particular way of thinking. It is not possible to maintain a façade for a prolonged period of time and it is dishonest to lead a client into the belief that we accept them when in fact we experience great hatred toward them. We have spoken mostly regarding the relationship that we have toward our clients regarding congruence but our genuine relationships with other people start with a genuine relationship with ourselves. Rollo May (1989) States:

Deceit of others and self-deceit go hand in hand. In fact, a person who did not deceive himself or herself to some degree could not long continue to deceive others, as he or she would recognise the folly of the trick. Both kinds of deceit may succeed temporarily, but only to fail the more disastrously in the end, precisely because they are deceit. The more penetrating ones insight into the deep workings of personality, the more one is convinced of the uselessness of trying to fool either oneself or others.
The Art of Counselling by Rollo May (1989)

The ego states of Parent, Adult and child exist within all of us and are triggered by our encounters with other people. Our ego states also interact with each other inside our own mind. For example our parent ego may constantly criticise us. Being overly self-critical is a sign of a strong 'Parent ego; however the individual who is unable to live up to the requirements of a critical parent ego will find that they spend most of their time in Adapted child dealing with emotions of inadequacy. You will hear some people boast that they are perfectionists and perhaps they have learned to be perfect to pacify their own neurotic tendency to experience self-loathing when failure occurs. Fooling ourselves can become a terrible habit that we become so used to that we forget that that it is a lie. We can see in history the most evil crimes during the witch burning times and inquisition was committed by people who truly believed that they were compassionate. Congruence requires that all beliefs and values are in harmony. If our beliefs are in conflict with each other then we cannot hope to develop self-esteem or self-actualise. Self-esteem requires that we must have an accurate self-concept and value the qualities that make up that concept. People who have conflicting values cannot have high self-esteem because they are in a constant state of conflict which involves self condemnation as incongruities enter into awareness.

How can we truly value who we are if we spend our time putting on a façade? Without congruence the other conditions for growth may not develop. Jan Sutton and William Stewart stated in their book learning to counsel:

"Genuiness (congruence) is the precondition for empathy and unconditional positive regard. Effective counselling depends wholly on the degree to which the counsellor is integrated and genuine."
Learning to Counsel by Jan Sutton and William Steward (2008)

Becoming aware of our incongruities is the only avenue to developing the following conditions of 'Unconditional positive regard' and 'empathy.' These are two qualities that are just as easily misunderstood as congruence. We will now discuss the quality of 'Positive regard.'

Unconditional Positive Regard.

From a counselling point of view 'Positive regard' is closely related to the social stage of Maslow's Hierarchy of Needs. Its quality effects the development of self-esteem needs and it is from this stage we measure the extent of our personal value based on our interactions with other people. Positive regard is offered in two ways either conditionally or unconditionally. The difference between the two is vast. 'Conditional' positive regard is acceptance or love that is offered with strings attached. The conditions of worth that we have already discussed are extremely important if we hope to gain acceptance from an authority or parental figure. As a child, it is love we need more than anything else. Without love we will never develop as a well-adjusted human being. We need the love of our parents or they will neglect us or perhaps even abandon us. Neglect and abandonment are issues closely related to 'Safety Needs' but we are assuming that a child has not been completely rejected but rather that there is physical safety needs are provided for, but their ability to attract love and belonging is paid for by giving up autonomy. Unconditional positive regard is a rather academic way of saying 'unconditional love' but it does describe the meaning quite well. It means acceptance of an individual without judgment regarding their character or actions but rather accept them in an unattached way, allowing them the freedom to grow in their own unique way, with their own beliefs and values; without the tendency to guide, interpret or evaluate the client's world. The unattached relationship requires that the professional is able to keep maintain boundaries and the family member is able to distinguish their own values from another's without feeling aggrieved if they are not the same.

To accept someone as valuable despite their perceived inadequacies can be extremely difficult for some people. Our acceptance of people we meet can be very much based on our own introjects. When unconditional positive regard is offered the message is "I give you the freedom to have your own feelings and experiences and apply your own meaning to them," It is a state of caring for someone rather than an attitude of, "I care for you if you behave in such n such a way". Unconditional positive regard cannot be offered to or clients unless we have developed the same attitude toward our own 'self'. This means that we must have transcended social needs and also experience fulfilled esteem needs. If you do not accept yourself unconditionally how could you accept another? If you apply perfectionist rules to yourself, how could you offer anything but rules for attaining 'unconditional positive regard?' This is why congruence is so important. To have addressed our own state of incongruence affords us the self-awareness and self-acceptance to accept a client unconditionally. We can pretend to offer unconditional regard and hide our disapproval of a client's feelings and beliefs but this will become obvious as the loss of positive regard and congruence makes it impossible to experience empathy.

Empathy.

Empathy is often misunderstood. Empathy is the tendency to sense another's world as if it was your own but realising that it is 'actually not'. It requires willingness to 'bracket off' our own model of the world, in effect ask it to sit in the corner and be quiet so that the client's beliefs, talents, experiences and social roles can be focused upon to stimulate accuracy. It is not a psychic experience or an expression of compassionate understanding; rather it is a natural emotional experience based purely on our observations. I say 'purely on our observations' because if we contaminate the process with correlations to our own similar experiences then we will lose empathy because we will confuse their experience with our own. People who are caught in their 'nurturing parent ego' are usually not able to experience empathy but rather they will offer sympathy. Sympathy is the tendency to look at another's situation from our own 'frame of reference.' The words, "I know how you feel because the same thing happened to me," has no meaning because everyone has different perceptions of a situation. Bereavement is a classic example of how our emotional experiences are different. Sarah was asked to counsel a woman who had lost her husband to cancer. Sarah felt she was the best person to counsel this woman because she also lost her husband to cancer some years ago. As the woman spoke of sitting with her husband during those last breaths Sarah could feel the emotion inside herself like a bubble about to burst, she really felt she had a deeper empathy with the poor widow because of their similar situation. Just as Sarah began to allow the tears fall from her eyes she expressed, "I understand what you are going through, because I have experienced the same thing." The widow looked at Sarah with joy and they held hands with a connection that felt so deep to Sarah that it could have been almost spiritual, and then the widow said, "That's wonderful. I have always felt guilty for taking joy in his death, I really hated him, and I just know it's wrong to think badly of the dead." The widow had experienced many years in a loveless marriage where verbal abuse was the norm. She felt joy and freedom when her husband died but needed to come to terms with the feeling of guilt that the joy brought. Sarah was completely taken aback. She had imposed her own similar experience of loss onto the widow and erroneously labelled it 'Empathy.' This had further implications for her counselling relationship because Sarah was now offended and lost 'positive regard'. Sarah had made the mistake of self disclosing and falling into her own 'Frame of reference.' She thought to herself, "I loved my husband. How could she think I could hate him?" Sarah felt misunderstood; it was as if the widow was being disrespectful to Sarah's own grief but Sarah had been too focused on her own grief to understand the widow's feelings of guilt. Some counsellors claim to have a deeper empathy with people who have similar issues as their own, but this perspective is nonsense as it is most likely cause more confusion and misunderstanding of another's world. Counsellors and psychotherapists go through continuous personal development to put their own experiences to rest so that they can listen to another's storey without being brought into back into their own. It is essential to be able to 'bracket off' our own 'stuff' if we hope to be an effective practitioner. Erving & Miriam Polster state:

"In bracketing-off, the individual holds some of his own concerns in abeyance in favour of attending to what is going on in a commutative process... bracketing off, one is established priorities as to what is most important at that time and not allowing interfering concerns to immobilise him."

Gestalt Therapy Intergrated by Erving & Miriam Polster (1973) Page 43

Empathy is nothing more than an interpretation and its accuracy should not be taken for granted but rather it needs to be confirmed through feedback. A human baby cries when it is in distress. An inexperienced parent can despair when feeding and changing the child's nappy does not calm the infant's cries. Obviously a baby could not cry for fun or to be mischievous so there must be a problem that has not been identified. Parents can become distracted by their own need for sleep or other concerns and find it difficult to use the natural empathic ability to get an idea of a baby's need. The baby can sense the stress in the parents breathing and instinctively reacts in the same way. Is mother in danger? Am I in danger? The reaction is understandable. It is only by using feedback from the child that we can find out if our empathic reaction has been accurate and sometimes this can only be achieved through practice and experience. Quite often it is the grandma who recognises the problem and applies a well-rehearsed pat on the back to help bring up the wind or just a hug with calm breathing and singing quietly in their ear can bring about the feeling of safety and a return to sleep. Empathy gets stronger with practice, and is a lesson in humility. If the human infant witnesses the stressful emotions of another they will immediately reflect what it instinctively recognises. In a room full of babies, if one cries you can bet that some others will follow suit to a grand chorus of crying babies. This is an instinctive reaction called emotional contagion. Of course it's fair to say that a baby does not emulate someone else's cries through any understanding of their world because the baby has little or no understanding of anything outside their own experience; they are in effect a blank slate without contamination from experience or the ability to evaluate their experience. When Grandma hugs the baby, the feeling of her chest breathing calmly, and the sound of her quiet singing brings about empathic/ emotional contagion. The baby senses the calmness and safety grandmas breathing brings and begins to sleep. To experience empathy we must be prepared to be the same and the only way to do this is to leave our evaluations out of our awareness so we can learn from feedback. In order to receive feedback we must make observations regarding the subtle body language, changes in voice tone and speed as well as the emotive words spoken and present them to the client for them to clarify the emotions. Bringing the clients unconscious expressions to their attention offers them the opportunity to put a meaning to them and increase their own awareness regarding their emotions; it requires no guess work from the practitioner. This is an opportunity for the practitioner to demonstrate that they are not judging the client or expecting them to agree with their interpretation of their emotion, but rather it demonstrates that the client is accepted unconditionally and that the practitioner is motivated by genuine non possessive positive regard and not by ego. Properly expressed, Empathy is the ultimate expression of genuiness/congruence and unconditional positive regard. Some books will advocate an expression of intuition with our clients but the problem with this is that intuition is not a given and is not always accurate, it can actually express non acceptance and an egoistic attempt to fish for credibility. It can be contaminated by a great many experiences and beliefs from our own past. Malcolm Gladwell (2005) states:

"Our unconscious is a powerful force. But it's fallible. It is not the case that our internal computer always shines through, instantly decoding the "truth" of a situation. It can be thrown off, distracted, and disabled. Our instinctive reactions often have to compete with all kinds of other interests and emotions and sentiments."
Blink By Malcolm Gladwell (2005) Published By Penguin Page 15

The ability to experience emotions by observing another person assists us through life. Empathy is much more accurate when people have rapport. Rapport is achieved when two people are locked in communication with a deep connection and understanding. People with the same values, beliefs and goals will be observed talking with each other by mirroring each other's body language and voice tone. This type of rapport can be seen between client and counsellor demonstrating a good rapport between the two. The difference between a social interaction and the counselling relationship is that the therapist is aware that that rapport has been established and cleverly uses techniques to stimulate this rapport. Establishing empathy and assisting the client to understand and accept their own emotions is enhanced by the use of mirroring and matching while in dialogue. In a natural setting people who have a deep connection can be seen adopting the same posture and stance. They will also make similar gestures, take a sip of coffee at the same time, tilt there head in the same way. It is almost beautiful to watch people making such a deep dance of connection. The counsellor will be aware that if they subtly emulate such behaviour with a client that they can bring the client into rapport with some ease and even if it is difficult to get an understanding of the client's world that it is possible to at least make the client feel accepted unconditionally until empathy is fully established. By observing the clients body language to a point where we are mirroring it we can more easily experience the changes in emotions that the client does not express verbally. Observation of a client's non-verbal indicators are the most accurate indicators of their mood, words can be misleading. When working in care and support with people who have learning disabilities it is extremely important to be able to anticipate the service users' needs by use of empathic observation. We can observe differences in walking, breathing, fidgeting, withdrawal that all appear to indicate that there is something wrong. By being empathically vigilant our service users can have their needs fulfilled before any challenging behaviour occurs. Empathy assists the practitioner to anticipate the client's mood and accurately understand the purpose for those feelings and can also indicate avenues of growth for the service user. A 'service user' in care and support maybe unfulfilled by their activities. I was aware of a day centre service user with learning disabilities who displayed challenging behaviour by being disruptive and occasionally violent. His behaviour had been addressed by authoritarian measures by carers who could not distinguish between 'parent ego' and 'adult ego,' and as a result he was 'told off' and told to conform to the support workers code of conduct. He was required to sit and be quiet but he couldn't sustain calm behaviour for long and his day was spent between the behaviours of disruption and grudgingly sitting quiet. He was eventually introduced to a support worker who was prepared to look at things from his frame of reference and got a sense that his behaviour was a 'need to express energy,' and so was enrolled on outdoor walking activities. After only one day of entering into his new activities his challenging behaviour stopped and only returned on days when he was unable to attend his activities due to weather conditions. In this scenario taking a Humanistic/Person Centred Approach brought about major improvements individuals well-being. The contrast from his previous experience was vast. Instead of being told to conform to the service, the service was now adjusting to his needs. The ingredients for this were:

A Genuine/ congruence: A professional who was committed to personal development.
Unconditional Positive Regard: expressed by re-framing challenging behaviour as an expression of need.
Empathy: Expressed by recognising the behaviour as a way of expressing discontent.
This service user was motivated to behave in a challenging way by his 'Actualising tendency,' with a view to fulfilling a need, but it wasn't until he entered into a supportive social environment that his social needs were met. This service user's behaviour improved and his health appeared to improve as a result of his new environment. It appeared that it was a result of a new support worker being introduced into his life that he was able to move toward a greater sense of well-being. We can only have our needs fulfilled if our environment supports this. As a professional we create an environment by means of our attitude.

The Hierarchy of Needs.

Our needs are progressive, unless we have completed the previous stage we cannot hope to transcend to the next; however once we have transcended to the next stage there is greater tolerance of deprivation and higher needs such as personal goals and ethical ideals can be placed in priority. This can be witnessed in people who will sacrifice food, safety and 'social belonging needs' for something they believe is important such as being a member of a political reform movement that threatens their social stability or employment, charitable work in a war torn land that puts you in danger, or risking death by walking to the South Pole. Once we have transcended certain needs our higher esteem and actualisation needs can take the priority and be the dominating force in life. This can be an effect of both directions of the social stage; whether we move toward 'self actualisation' or 'actualising an ideal.' For example someone who bases their self-esteem upon the approval of family and peers may sacrifice their safety by becoming a suicide bomber. The direction of actualisation is therefore vital if the individual is going to develop autonomously and independently of persuasion. In the westernised world we will find that most people have no need to worry about the more basic needs because they are easily fulfilled by supermarkets and welfare systems in times of crisis; but in some lands fulfilling the basic needs for food and water and safety is difficult to accomplish.

Basic Physiological Needs:

It is very rare to meet anyone in the west who does not have their need for food and water fulfilled' however this can happen in affluent western lands such as the UK and

USA due to mental illness, disability, alcohol/drug addiction and neglect of dependants. It has been reported that in some rare cases that care homes and hospitals for the elderly have neglected their duty of care for dependant residence who have become malnourished and dehydrated; but generally speaking residential care services provide not only an excellent provision in caring for residence basic needs but also the commitment to fulfilling higher needs. Care homes, day centres and other supporting services will provide basic needs such as food and liquid in the way the service user wants it. It would be a form of abuse to provide a take or leave it policy to people who are completely dependent on a service. I worked in a UK day centre which had a policy of encouraging choice as a means of encouraging esteem needs. At lunch time there was an abundance of choice of salads, fish meat pies and curry dishes as well as quality beverages. This day service didn't have set meal times but rather could have lunch when they pleased. This extremely popular service allowed people to arrange activities without the worry of missing lunch time. The only reason that a service user would to think about food was when making a choice about what to eat. To a great extent people in affluent lands take their provision for food and water for granted and we would probably find it difficult to relate to the obsessional thoughts that deprivation brings. Psychiatrist Viktor Frankl (1959) describes his own experience of starvation in the Nazi concentration Camps, He states:

What did the prisoner dream about most frequently? Of bread, cake, cigarettes, and nice warm baths. The lack of having these simple desires satisfied led him to wish-fulfilment in dreams… Because of the high degree of undernourishment which the prisoner suffered, it was natural that the desire for food was the natural primitive instinct around which mental life centred.
Man's Search for Meaning Vicktor E. Frankl. (1959) p40, 41

Throughout human history humans have been under constant threat of extinction due to famine and ice ages. Our large powerful brains require vast amounts of calories to keep us functioning and as result our thinking was focussed on developing ingenious ways of hunting. For most of our history we were nomads who obtained food by hunting and gathering. On cave walls we find depictions of animals, the food of ancient man. After humans invented agriculture and living in communities' food became less of a priority of mind and humans were able to focus upon learning. Within six thousand years of becoming farmers the human race had developed moderate empires with pyramids, irrigation systems, writing and mathematics. All of these developments are expressions of higher needs that could not be accomplished without first transcending the basic physiological needs.

I feel it is important to also mention the importance of the social needs during this stage. It has been mentioned earlier that without love it is unlikely that any child or dependant would survive as they rely on being cared for and it is true that in the nomadic times before humans lived in farming communities that we have cave paintings that demonstrate that <u>hunting was also a social activity</u> which contributed to our survival as a species. The provision of all human needs appears to be centred on our social support even though we do not count this as important to our survival as food. Humans appear to innately place great emphasis on social needs as part of our survival and may sacrifice the basic needs in favour of providing social support to kith and kin. Vicktor Frankl described witnessing this in the concentration camps.

It had been a bad day. On parade, an announcement had been made about the many actions that would, from then on, be regarded as sabotage and therefore punishable by immediate death by hanging. Among these were crimes such as cutting small strips from our old blankets (in order to improvise ankle supports) and very minor "thefts." A few days previously a semi-starved prisoner had broken into the potato store to steal a few pounds of potatoes. The theft had been discovered and some prisoners had recognized the "burglar." When the camp authorities heard about it they ordered that the guilty man be given up to them or the whole camp would starve for a day. Naturally the 2,500 men preferred to fast.
<u>Man's Search for Meaning Vicktor E. Frankl. (1959) p88</u>

It could be argued that these men had already transcended the basic needs before entering the concentration camps and were self-actualised; exercising their ethical autonomy, or that there was social pressure to keep quiet. With the pain of starvation and exhaustion combined with the constant obsessive thoughts of food it was certainly a transient stance to take to choose to suffer to protect a fellow human. This attitude was probably an expression of esteem needs in relation to personal ethics but certainly this would have been against the physical urge of the body's natural mechanisms to survive.

We know that people can fight their natural drive to eat but one physiological drive that we cannot control is the need for sleep, if we fight it; it will eventually win. A child who gets a good night's rest is assured to be ready for school and will fare better than a child who goes to school fatigued. People who suffer from stress are robbed of sleep and find thinking to be a difficult task. Sleep deprivation reduces the effectiveness on almost all aspects of human life, but humans don't always appreciate its importance. George's performance at work fell considerably and neither he nor his colleagues could identify the problem. He was not only slowing in production but also making embarrassing mistakes. He was sent to see the company counsellor who identified that his performance had begun to slip around his birthday. They both discussed this time in his life and although he had turned 40 there was no other reason for his work to be slipping. His sleep pattern appeared to suggest that he was suffering from stress, some nights he would not sleep at all and he would come to work irritable and tired. The answer was simple but not obvious. He had not suffered a bereavement or relationship break up. He had not suffered a trauma or financial ruin. The reason that he couldn't sleep and his work was going down the tube was down to nothing more than excessive Caffeine. On George's birthday, his mum bought him an espresso machine which made the most beautiful cup of coffee. All night before he went to bed and in the morning before he went to work he would make a nice latte with a triple espresso and then another and then another. Being a counsellor can sometimes be about detective work and looking for the obscure. You certainly don't need to talk through your caffeine problems but it wasn't until he spoke to his counsellor that he was able to identify the probable cause of his insomnia. George simply stopped drinking coffee and his sleep pattern returned to normal as did his effective work. Of course stress is a very real cause of sleep deprivation and people who suffer from stress will naturally find that their thoughts keep them awake at night as they run scenarios through their minds that trigger their autonomic nervous system, but the caffeine effect does exactly the same thing so differentiating the two can be difficult.

One of the most neglected needs that humans experience is the needs for physical exercise. The human body is a very fuel efficient system which will store energy as fat. For service users in care and support; there needs to be a provision of physical exercise if they are to maintain health. Certainly it would be abuse not to provide the opportunity to exercise. I have seen some institutions commit to mixing exercise with creativity during their day, these are very inspiring places. I had the privilege of working in a day centre that provided 'wheelchair aerobics. ' many of the service users reported an increase in a sense of well-being after each session. I have also seen the neglect of day centres for people with learning disabilities that warehoused physically able people into rooms with nothing to stimulate them physically except a colouring book and crayon. The physical need for exercise is an important aspect. If an individual is placed into an environment where their need for food is more than adequately catered for but they are confined to a wheelchair, then it is likely that they will consume more calories than they will use. The experience for many individuals who are wheelchair users is that they very quickly put weight on. This can cause further difficulty in mobility and attending to their own personal needs. Exercise in the form of wheel chair aerobics or attending a gym helped many feel that they were at least taking control of the situation. Sport can not only fulfil physical needs but also some social needs as people feel they belong to a team. Physical exercise can also contribute toward combating stress. Many of my counselling clients express that they find visiting the gym or going for a good run alleviates stress. It could be that the stress hormones that are pumping around their system have found an outlet. For people who work in an office where physical activity is minimal the sense of stress can be quite high especially if caffeine is drank to excess. Stress leads us into the safety needs.

Safety Needs

A feeling of safety means we experience peace, freedom from harm. This is accomplished when we have a space that protects us from the harsh weather and potential predators. People who have been camping in a flimsy tent often speak of the vulnerability they feel sleeping in a tent where the only thing between them and the 'mad knifed attacker' is a flimsy piece of canvas. Our safety is an instinctive need but it is not always about sleeping in a safe brick house or carrying a tazer gun for protection. It is very difficult to relax circumstances where we feel unsafe. The safety needs involve security and predictability. As we have already discussed sleep deprivation can be caused by stress. The reason for this is a logical one. If we are unsafe we need to find a solution to our problem, so the mind will not focused upon nice things like butterflies and kittens but will rather focus on creating solutions to a problem by running different scenarios that will prepare for any threat that may arise. The process of imagining negative scenarios and preparing a solution contributes to a sense of predictability and a sense of security. If problems are easy to solve then sleep will come easy, but if a problem threatens your relationships, your health or your finances you may find that your mind focuses open finding a solution. Any threat will raise levels of stress because our safety is compromised. With high stress levels comes hyper vigilance and also negative thinking which has evolved to predict the potential scenario's that could result personal damage. Every time we imagine something negative we feel the stress as if it is happening in the present. If we vividly imagine being chased by an elephant then we may feel the excitement that it creates as our muscles tense. If you are worried about being a passenger in your bosses car because you know he has a sever visual impairment then you might feel the tension and fear as you imagine the car being driven off the road and off a cliff face. The experience of stress is a clear indication that somebody feels that their safety needs have not been fulfilled. This does not mean that their thoughts represent reality but it does dictate whether they will transcend to the next stage of the hierarchy of needs. If an individual is to have their safety needs fulfilled then they must have a sense of security and the ability to predict positive or at least peaceful outcomes. The safety needs require an individual to feel that they can protect their interests and maintain a continuous state of resourcefulness that will defend them against adversity. It may include having a secure job with enough money and a secure home. In human history it would be the reassurance that there were plenty resources in the environment to sustain life or the security knowing that there is someone who knows how to start a fire to keep warm. The ability to build dwellings that could shelter humans from the elements and also store food over the winter months would also bring much needed safety. Human intelligence has sustained the human race. In every community there has always been someone who is able to use reasoning and knowledge to sustain the group. Social intelligence and diplomacy has not only assisted human groups not to kill each other but to support each other through trade of supplies and skills. Education is therefore one of the most important developments in human history for our continued security and safety. We see children encouraged to learn at school so they can have a secure future by attracting the best paid job with a company pension. It is well known that it is the most educated men in all of history that have saved communities by their understanding of fire, invention of the spear, organisation of agriculture and development of trade. These humans recognised that the movement of the sun and the stars correlate to the seasons and erected great monuments to measure and follow the sun during the year and from this came the ability to measure time and predict the seasons and the available foods that are available during those seasons. The security that this knowledge brought must have drawn people to the new towns and cities which were not only able to supply their own food but also use their abundance to trade with other communities who emulated their practices and were able to further contribute to the security of their population. Without wanting to push the historical development of the human race too much we can certainly see that our security needs as a species has been fulfilled by our intelligence and the continuous building upon knowledge that we as humans are committed to through our educational systems. It is very true that the most affluent lands value education and the poorest and most deprived countries either suppress education or do not provide any at all. The resourcefulness that Education brings many benefits to our security needs. Some people are so dependant on supermarkets that if they were all to close tomorrow they would starve or resort to stealing, but the intelligent individual would plan ways of finding food through hunting or rearing their own animals to produce milk and eggs. This type of situation was seen during the Second World War. Some people would sacrifice food tokens in favour of keeping their own animals to produce food and as a result fared well by sustaining their own families and making money from selling their surplus. As a child our safety needs are fulfilled by our parents who bring a sense of security. We are provided with a house and routines such as meal times that provide us with a sense of peace. Well cared for children don't need to think about their safety because they are rarely faced with danger. The importance of safety to a child can be seen when they think they have lost their mother in a supermarket, the panic in a child's face as they cry for help is comparable to the terror you would expect from someone who is about to be killed but this is understandable. Most of our history has taken place as nomad tribesmen who were constantly on the move to the next fertile area, if a child was lost, it would be most likely be an unfamiliar area with the prospect of death from exposure to the elements or being eaten being very likely. Working with people who are dependant requires a sense of routine and predictability to make them feel secure. A child finds security in familiar faces, meal times and increasing development of survival based knowledge. Abandonment is a very real threat to the child. Even if one parent disappears from their life they may find that their security is reduced. A child will feel stress when hearing parents arguing with each other as family break up will create serious issues for the child regarding who will care for them. In ancient times it was a potential death sentence for a mother to be abandoned by her husband. To care for infants and gather enough food to sustain everyone would be almost impossible without support. This is well illustrated by the Bible account of Abraham's abandonment of Hagar and Ishmael in Genesis 21.

Abraham took some bread and a skin of water and, giving them to Hagar, put the child on her shoulder and sent her away. She wandered off into the desert of Beersheba. When the skin of water was finished she abandoned the child under a bush. Then she went and sat down at a distance, about a brow shot away, thinking, "I cannot bear to see the child die." Sitting at a distance she began to sob.
New Jerusalem Bible: Genesis 21:14-16

In ancient times the threat of being banished from a community was not something that could be treat as a mild punishment, it meant being without support and the prospect of malnourishment and exposure to the harsh elements. If a child witnesses parents in conflict then their fear of abandonment will be very instinctive and very real. Supporting people in care also needs to include predictability and familiarity to avoid stress and challenging behaviour. This does not mean that there should never be spontaneity or regular change but rather that the individual has an awareness of what to expect in the near future and that the event includes activities that the service user feels able to adapt to without feeling abandoned. For many service users the knowing when and where food will be obtained from, who will be supporting and the ease of access to toilet facilities will be of primary importance. For people who have complex disabilities quite often a familiar support worker will provide them with a sense of safety because their needs are understood due to the worker being familiar and able to assist them without causing embarrassment. For some service users who have complex needs, visiting the bathroom with a support worker who is unfamiliar with your needs can be a traumatic experience so it is important that a service user works with varied staff so they can feel secure that when their main support worker is off work with the flue that there is an abundance of other staff who can adequately attend to their needs. Physical and emotional safety are quite often glossed over but the effect of stress caused by insecurity is a significant reason people seek counselling and psychotherapy. For people who spend their life in supported care it can appear impossible to ask them to cooperate with change or make progress toward making goals; however, understanding the service users need for a sense of security we can encourage advancement by using support plans that borrow ideas from 'life coaching', to devise a structured set of small goals that are devised and controlled by the service user. The safety that a service user feels when supported to create their own activities and goals assist them to feel the security to plan increasingly advanced goals in the future which can lead to some amazing results such as shopping for their self and paying with their own money. Some service users in supported care have even made progressive goals toward employment. These goals can seem unrealistic until they are broken down into stress free chunks.

People who suffer domestic abuse find themselves locked in a world where their thoughts and behaviour are conditioned by the verbal and physical threats of an abuser. In this situation the victim becomes nothing more than an object that is owned. Safety is such a significant need that humans will conform to the demands of an abuser to preserve the well-being of their self and of their families. When in an argument with someone or shouting at a child the aim is to use the critical parent to make them retreat into adapted child; in effect make them adapt to the will of the critical parent ego. In such circumstance the one who submits does so, not because the other person has won an argument but rather because the other person has evoked enough fear in their opponent that they submit to their authority in order to preserve safety. At this point we also cross into the social needs which obviously involve our experiences regarding our value which are communicated throughout the basic and safety needs. To transcend the safety needs we must feel as if we are human rather than an object or a burden to be endured; we must be communicated with and it is this communication that contributes to the transcendence from safety needs to Social Needs.

Social Needs

For humans there is nothing more important than love and belonging. To be accepted by your family and community is something that we would assume is a given. Our basic and safety needs are fulfilled because we were loved by our parents and accepted by the wider community. But if we need to be accepted by our families in order for our most basic needs to be fulfilled, why are social needs placed at number three of the hierarchy of needs and not at the beginning before the basic physiological needs? Certainly, you will not die without love if food and safety are present; but children who experience social deprivation will fail to develop in a normal way. The studies of feral children who have been isolated or abandoned until their teens have been found to display sever developmental problems involving speech and motor functions. An example of this was 'Genie' who was locked in a room and immobilised by being strapped to a cot or children's toilet until the age of thirteen. It could be argued that the girls 'safety needs' were the issue but generally speaking she was deprived because she was in an environment where she was not accepted or loved. After her rescue she never developed normal speech and found simple motor skills such as walking difficult because she had missed critical periods in neurological development. It is normal part of life that we learn to talk through observation and mimicry, we learn to walk through continuous attempts to balance and move in the direction of those people who love and value us with our arms open wide. Without encouragement and an object of love the baby would have very little joy in its achievements. The power of love and acceptance is given little attention by empirical studies because it is difficult to define and quantify; but we are all aware how it felt to sit on a merry-go-round and see our mother wave to us; or when we had a small part in the school play to see our mothers face in the crowed beaming with pride. To be valued by our parents is something a child desires more than anything else. I remember at the end of my sons nativity play all the parents were invited to say hello to their children and take photos. The children smiled and introduced their friends to their mum and dad with pride. In every school there is the child who sits alone because his or her parents have not made the time to attend, perhaps they have work commitments or other pressures but a child's self-evaluation will be active during these times and they will feel the hurt and internalise the non-attendance as a measure of their worth in comparison to the joy of their friends. Parents who view their child's achievements as unimportant are robbing them of personal validation. Validation reinforces the belief that we are accepted and safe. It tells us our place in other people's lives and also allows us to relax knowing that you are a valuable individual and most of all wanted. A child who is trying to get their parents attention while they spin around the merry-go-round will eventually stop waving to their mother and give her a break from the constant exercise when their need for validation is satisfied. Some children will stop waving because their mother is not watching them at all, but is instead texting someone on Facebook, describing how lovely their lunch looks. The child in such circumstances evaluates themselves on how much interest is shown towards them. Social needs are a need for validation and a sense of value from others. When we receive gifts, a hand shake or a simple hello in the street we become validated as people, we are acknowledged as existing. Stroking is a term used in transactional analysis to describe the act of acknowledging another's existence. This can be done verbally or physically. It can be accomplished by listening to someone intently and sending them a card or gift. Stroking is desired because we crave validation but strokes can be painful as well as soothing. A positive stroke is the kind we desire; words of praise, shaking of your hand, or a friendly smile, a bunch of flowers. Negative strokes are acknowledgement such as a good telling off or physical chastisement. In the absence of a positive stroke a negative stroke will suffice to fulfil the need although the evaluation from a negative stroke is generally unpleasant but it is at least an acknowledgement that you exist. To invalidate somebody is to discount their strokes or request for acknowledgement. We have already discussed how this can happen without direct intention between a parent and a child but it can be seen happening in care. Someone in who is physically dependant on care from professionals needs to be acknowledged if they are to maintain a sense of self-worth, this is a reason why the social needs are present during the other previous stages, but they have their prominent influence when transcending to esteem needs.

We will now look at how fulfilling social needs regarding use of strokes, enhances the quality of the other needs for a service user in a day centre.

Gerry suffered a stroke when he was 58 and as a result became badly immobilised and lost his ability to communicate verbally. He was placed into day care during his rehabilitation. Due to his inability to speak and limited movements he was unable to inform staff when he needed to visit the bathroom. It was difficult to attract the attention of staff at his day centre because they were always being called to tend to the needs of other service users. Gerry would frequently soil himself as a result of being unable to call staff attention and felt humiliated when his accident was discovered when staff were informed about the smell by other service users. The experience of being bathed when the situation could have been prevented was frustrating and annoying for Gerry who began to lash out at the staff for not checking on his needs. His violent behaviour was reported to his social worker who asked for a report on the circumstances around the incident. The report suggested that Gerry was incontinent and that Gerry should be issued with incontinence pads. Gerry was obviously in an environment that ignored him he was discounted and was in effect abandoned. The effect on his self-esteem was appalling. He had a history of working in management positions and had the respect of every employee who he came into contact with. He had fathered 4 children who all went to university and his wife adored him. Now he felt like nothing more than a burden to the care service and felt ashamed because of an incident that happened because he was neglected. It was discovered that the staff had not made themselves familiar with his support plan which stated that Gerry uses a picture board to communicate and is able to write single words with his right hand if given a pen and white board. The staff needed to increase their awareness of Person Centred Values beyond the need to fulfil paper work and risk assessments but also regarding the development of humanistic attitudes. The whole service was transformed by the development of the staff and the well-being of all service users was improved. There were a lot of issues involved in Gerry's situation, certainly his basic and safety needs were not fulfilled in this day centre; however with the introduction of the Person Centred Values meant that Gerry and other service users had their need for strokes fulfilled by constant communication and staff observing non-verbal cues that a service user may need attention. Gerry's situation involved the deprivation of:

- Basic physiological needs: No hydration.

- Safety needs: Inability to predict if personal needs will be attended and fear of humiliation. Discomfort and stress caused by the expectation of neglect.

- Social Needs: No communication or acknowledgement. Invalidated by staff who discount needs.

- Esteem needs: He was adapting to a social role that was not valued and was applying that evaluation to self. No choices or preferences presented to him. Food and times of lunch were on a take or leave it basis. Unable to communicate desired activities that he would desire to be involved in.

Gerry was able to communicate the reality by using a pencil . Ignoring the fact that the complaint that was logged and the consequent compensation payment; Gerry's situation immediately changed. He was now regularly acknowledged by staff and asked if he needed anything.

Gerry not only was able to go to the toilet when he desired but he was also able to ask for a drink when required and was assisted to alter his sitting position if he had become uncomfortable. Gerry situation had changed from losing hope developing depression and reduced sense of self-worth to a situation where he was valued by staff that made his well-being a priority. The improved communication with Gerry enabled staff to identify activities that would occupy him and it was discovered that his limited mobility enabled him to take part in board games and carpet sports. The philosophical attitude of the professionals was pivotal in supplying a supportive environment and after the social worker encouraged a review of his support plan the manager of the day centre arranged for his staff to receive more supervision and personal development workshops.

Unconditional Positive Regard facilitated the process of stroking. It is through the process of stroking that we communicate that we truly value someone. As we saw with Gerry's situation, he began to re-evaluate his own value based on his perceived social role and the behaviour of others toward Gerry, in a powerful position. Humans cannot help but evaluate 'self' based on the reactions of others toward them. In counselling and psychotherapy the therapist will offer unconditional positive regard as a means of demonstrating that the client is accepted as a human being with equal default potential and abilities as every other human. The difficulty that many clients experience is that they introject the conditions of worth from significant others in their life and use this as a guide to behaviour and thinking. It is at this stage that an individual will begin on their voyage of actualisation. The need for social bonding and the experience of love is extremely powerful, certainly it reinforces safety needs but it offers the individual the opportunity to learn to apply that acceptance to self and develop independence from others while maintaining a sense of value. The value of love is very instinctive; we can observe this social need in other mammals. Harry Harlow demonstrated that monkeys appear to have social needs and will suffer severe developmental problems if they are not allowed to interact with other monkeys from birth. Harlow's research involved isolating baby monkeys for varying periods of time and then introducing them to other monkeys. It was found that these monkeys would display strange behaviours and would display sever anxiety. One monkey refused to eat when introduced to other monkeys and died after five days. A comparison could be made the social and developmental problems exhibited by so called feral children such as Genie. Harlow went further and experimented to ascertain if bonding occurs due to the mother figure being viewed as a food source or if there is something more required. Harlow created two mothers for a baby monkey. One mother was made of wire and dispensed milk and the other mother was made of cloth. It was found that the wire mother was only approached for milk which fulfilled the monkey's basic physiological need; but would spend most of its time clinging to the cloth mother and when startled the monkey ran to the cloth mother for comfort rather than the provider. This appeared to suggest that there is something greater than the provision of food which contributes toward attachment. This need was not related to gaining food and liquid alone. Certainly, the issues that a client brings to a counselling session are normally related in some way to their relationships. Good relationships can assist us to cope with almost anything in life but the absence of this provision can also make life feel very uncertain. Nancy is woman in her late sixties and came for counselling because she was suffering from extreme loneliness. On closer investigation it appeared that she was actually experiencing grief. Her children had moved hundreds of miles away for career reasons and it was no longer practical to see each other any more than once every three months or so. She very much missed her grandchildren and felt that with the passage of time they would love her less. She so very much wanted to communicate with them, teach them how to cook, play games with them, but they were now not living anywhere near her. She was now socially isolated. This is a situation many older people deal with. Humans have survived near extinction because of our tendency to live in groups because it is within those groups that we are cared for and valued. The security that the group provides is only available if we are accepted. As already mentioned; there are religions that encourage a strong social bond between members with the threat to excommunicate any member who is disobedient to their rules and generally this is a successful form of mind control especially if the individual has no close contacts outside the church. The feeling of loss that Nancy felt was as great as loosing someone in death. She craved the distractions that company would bring. Eventually she joined a club for older people that included a drop in café and night time events. She developed close friendships and found that everyone naturally supported one another as best they could. The main benefit from this club was that she felt welcome and part of a community. In my experience, the reason most older people enter into day centres is for social interaction. The counsellor and psychotherapist are often visited by people who have a low opinion of self which has been learned through their interaction with other significant people in their life. People who have never had their need for positive regard fulfilled will constantly fish for approval. It is sad that many people will mould their lives based on their need for approval from others and waste their talents and potential. Barry was in a rock band and was offered the opportunity for a record deal but Barry's parents wanted him to go to university and become a lawyer. The desire to become a successful musician is strong, but he hungers for self-acceptance but trusts the judgement of others more and does not trust his own powers of evaluation. With a heavy heart he leaves the rock band to study law. After he graduates he finds a job as a receptionist at a local law firm and hates it, but has the satisfaction that his mother shows everyone who visits the house the wonderfully presented graduation photo. This makes him feel accepted. Matilda was encouraged by her parents to study maths at university so that she could become a teacher. She instead left education and started her own business selling coffee from a van. Her parents helped her research how this could be done and helped her financially to start the business. Matilda's parents were proud of her no matter what she chose to do, the difference between Barry and Matilda was that Matilda had unconditional positive self-regard and Barry was dependant on others to maintain a positive feeling regarding his worth.

Esteem needs

Having the esteem needs fulfilled is essential to the well-being of the individual if they ever hope to follow their own path and feel enough self-worth to speak in defence of themselves. Esteem or respect is something that we need to feel that we have purpose and value. It is the expression of an internal acceptance of self. When our esteem needs are fulfilled we may have experienced unconditional positive regard from people in our lives during the social stage and internalised that attitude and applied it to your self-concept. To have a trust and love of self is a great gift. We find many individuals who have high self-esteem are confident and secure. They appear to radiate safety and assurance because they truly trust their own abilities to find a solution or to offer something positive to the world. When someone accepts themselves unconditionally, it means that they are not ruled by introjects and conditions of worth. There are many people who have extremely low self-esteem normally due to their internalised conditions of worth that act as a guide to gaining the approval of others. People who make decisions based on the approval of other people are said to have an external locus of evaluation. An external locus of evaluation is a way of making a judgement using conditions of worth and introjects. Even when an individual is alone they may still solve a problem by asking themselves what someone else would do ion their situation. People with an external locus of evaluation are generally passive to the demands of others and could be termed 'people pleasers.' People pleasers have low self-esteem and fear rejection. Certainly they are constantly hungry for flattery or approval which makes them vulnerable to manipulation. People with low self-esteem are very easily manipulated and abused by people who would exploit their hunger for validation. This is something that is used by well-trained salesmen. People who are recruiting for charity are known for their manipulation of the general public. Mary received a phone call in the middle of the day and the caller asked her what she feels about the terrible disaster in Knotty Ash. Mary took the opportunity to create a wonderful image of herself to the caller by saying. "Eh, I think it's awful, all the kids without their mothers. It's heart breaking." Then the caller says "I don't know about you Mary, but it makes me feel really sick with compassion, I want to help in any way I can. If I could help I would help. Do you feel the same way? How does it make you feel?" For Mary it is a question that evokes her own need for esteem and she is starving for it. Mary jumps at the chance to be positively evaluated and agrees that she would do anything she could to help. This is when the caller offers her a wonderful opportunity to help. "Mary, I'm so pleased to hear you say that; because you can actually help and it won't involve flying to Knotty Ash, it's so much easier and yet you will actually be helping those kids. For Just £15 a month you will provide food and shelter for 20 children. How does that make you feel?" Mary doesn't want to make herself out to be a liar and sabotage her chance for some spoon fed admiration, so she responds, "eh, really good, I mean it's not much but I can afford it, and you know, I don't mind when I know it's helping the poor children of Knotty Ash." Mary commits herself to paying £15 a month and regrets it for a full six months before cancelling the direct debit. Mary finds that her need for esteem or respect is very strong and motivates most of her decision making. There are times when no one is around to help her make a decision and instead of trusting her own judgement, she asks herself, "What would mother have wanted me to do?" Mary's conditions of worth were abundant and she craved more and more rules to follow so that she could receive praise and respect. Mary's husband voted for the Labour Party, and so Mary also voted for the Labour Party. At work Mary would try to please the people that she viewed as in power and would constantly be on the lookout for things she could do to gain positive regard. She would lend large amounts of money to people and never get it back and as a result she would feel resentful, but kept quiet in order to maintain the image of a caring person that she wanted to be recognised for being. Mary was told by her Manager, "Mary I can always rely on you more than the other staff. Can I ask a favour, I know you have not had a day off for a month; but I really need you to work this weekend." Mary was exhausted and really wanted to spend time with her family and relax, but she didn't want to lose her managers respect and so she agreed and eventually developed sever stress symptoms. She missed quality time with her family, lost out financially and was becoming ill because she had no time for her own interests or to rest. Mary had a strong external locus of evaluation and this was making her ill. There is no doubt that having low self-esteem is a sure way to becoming nothing more than someone else's resource rather than a real person. We cannot be genuine if we constantly follow someone else's puppet or a robot that is waiting for instructions. In effect Mary is telling the world "I only matter if you approve of my existence." Mary is lost and doesn't know who she is. She has suppressed her own feelings and opinions for so long that she no longer values them or even knows they are there. Like all of us, Mary is an organism, and like all organism we have reactions, instincts feelings and preferences that is useful to be aware of. For example if we trust our natural organismic valuing system we will be protected from things like meat that has gone bad. All we have to do is smell meat that is rotting and our gagging reflex will become active to protect us from harm. Organismic valuing enables us to feel uneasy when meeting people who may threaten us in some way so that we could steer clear of them or make our excuses and leave their presence. Organismic valuing is very instinctive and will always be active, but for people like Mary it is suppressed and ignored in the attempt to gain peoples approval. To trust ones organism is to trust ones true self. Mary never listened to her organism as she agreed to work extra time at work, if she did then she would have been aware that her desire to have time off was not selfish but rather an essential need. If she had listened to her own anxiety and apprehension she would never have agreed to donate £15 a month to the Knotty Ash fund. Carl Rogers states:

We find, then, that there is a very real discrepancy between the experiencing organism as it exists, and the concept of self which exerts such a governing influence upon behaviour.

Client Centred Therapy : Carl R Rogers (1951) p510

Mary has in effect rejected herself in favour of an ego ideal. She wants to be respected for being helpful and compassionate but in the process of creating an unrealistic façade she suffers. Mary's esteem needs are not fulfilled and they will not be fulfilled until she is able to apply unconditional positive regard to herself, to love and respect her own needs.

Many people are passive to the will of others in order to receive respect, but they always end up being resentful and angry regarding their kind deeds as if the other person 'made them agree or else'. The passive individual is non-genuine, a fake, a phoney and a victim. The passive individual will lie. It sounds as if I am condemning people who are passive as immoral in some way but I am not. Passive people are all those things and in the end they suffer and the people around them never really get to know who they really are. It is interesting to watch a passive individual fluctuate between the parent and child ego states. Passive individuals have a very weak adult ego and as a result have difficulty becoming objective regarding their own experiences and are unable to experience true empathy, and so their communication with other people is often based on how they view themselves in comparison to the other individual. Mary was seen by her boss as helpful and keen to please him (adapted child). She was seen by her friends as caring but a bit off a gossip (nurturing and critical parent). Mary was asked to work with a new female student and train her to do some clerical work. Mary didn't like the look of the young student due to her Tattoos and piercings. Mary's boss was shocked to hear Mary shouting in the office and when he looked through the window he was shocked to see her yelling and pointing her figure at the student while holding a clump of A4 paper in her hand. The boss opened the door and asked if everything was all right and Mary threw her hands in the air and said "I'm dealing with a bad egg here, she can't even put paper in a photocopier," and then Mary walked out the office and down the corridor feeling a little embarrassed that her boss had found her behaving in an aggressive manner. Mary was unaware of her prejudice against the young student and felt safe to shout at her abusively, because she viewed herself a superior to her. She felt that aggression was the most appropriate way to demonstrate her authority. In effect Mary was using her critical parent to evoke the 'child' in the student and make her passive in an attempt to gain some sort of respect as the authority. Mary wanted the student to become passive with her in the same way that Mary was passive with her boss. Mary's fluctuation between passive and aggressive was based on her own reliance on a façade. Howard C.Cutler, MD States:

Many theorists see poor self-image and inflated-image as two sides of the same coin, conceptualising people's inflated self-image, for instance, as an unconscious defence against underlying insecurities and negative feelings about themselves.

The Art of Happiness: Howard C..Cutler. M.D. (1998).

Mary keeps her own needs out of awareness and is constantly playing a game of 'feed my ego with respect'. Mary's low self-esteem is caused by lack of awareness.

She knows what she thinks she should be, but she doesn't know who she actually is.

Mike is different. He is respected by everyone and he is always happy. He was asked by his boss to work overtime, but he just said 'no'. Mike offered no excuses, just a simple 'no.' Mike felt no guilt when he refused, and he knew he was going fishing with his son. As soon as we start giving people excuses, we are in effect asking to be excused in the same way a child will ask the teacher if the may leave to use the lavatory, and Mike won't do that he's got too much self-respect. His boss asked him what he was doing instead of over time in an attempt to embarrass him. His reply was simple, "I am pursuing other interests," His boss got the message and respected mike for his honesty. Mikes adult ego is his executive state. He respects himself and respects other people. He does not ask anyone to conform to his rules and has a great rapport with his boss and colleagues. He was asked to train a young student to use the photo copier, when he saw that she was struggling and becoming anxious when it chewed the paper he warmly laughed and offered reassurance. Because he was in his Adult ego state he was able to objectively experience empathy with the student and use this objectivity to control his 'nurturing parent' as a tool rather than a façade. Mike is genuine; he respects himself and offers unconditional positive regard to others. Mike has his esteem needs fulfilled because he has a strong internal locus of evaluation. He trusts his own organismic experience. If he feels anxious or uncertain he acknowledges this and contemplates why this is before making a decision. If he feels a desire to do something then he makes plans and does it. Mike has very little stress and due to his genuine approach to life.

In counselling and psychotherapy it is normal to find that people are struggling with self-esteem issues. Someone like Mary may visit a counsellor and express all her feelings of resentment and how life is a struggle before she begins to realise that she is responsible for creating her present situation and also for creating a new one. It can be a hard and long slog to become aware of our own true self if we have been suppressing it for so long that it has not been heard since childhood. For many clients simple dialogue will be sufficient to assist them to become more authentic. Awareness and responsibility are the keys to overcoming low self-esteem. For many of my clients I encourage mindfulness techniques to assist with organismic awareness. By focusing the mind on self process using an objective standpoint can assist an individual not only to become more aware of their own authentic experiences but also to accept them as part of self. In care and support the individual who is assisted to make choices regarding the T.V. they watch and the activities they are involved in. In a world where an individual in care is dependant on others to have their basic needs fulfilled it is important to offer esteem by demonstrating respect. This is not always obvious but ways this is accomplished is through good communication. An individual's esteem needs can be fulfilled when they are asked for permission before being bed bathed, or having personal needs attended to. Speaking to someone constantly to acknowledge they are a valuable individual to make sure that they are happy and comfortable can contribute to a sense of esteem. When we take notice of a service users support plan we may notice that they have cultural or religious preferences that need to be respected such as only eating certain foods, perhaps not being tended to by the opposite sex. By working within the clients boundaries of respect we can contribute toward fulfilling their esteem needs. Encouraging independence and supporting people to do things rather than doing it for them is a great way to encourage self-esteem. The most secure and happy children are the ones who have been shown how to do things rather than parents doing it for them. Some children are given regular opportunities to achieve and feel good about themselves by parents who encourage independence. Learning to tie your own shoe laces, make toast and use a telephone are all skills that assist a child to grow in confidence and esteem. We all want to see our children become all they can be. For the parent of a high self-esteem child there is pride and the ability to relax, knowing that they are capable of looking after themselves. Esteem needs are fully fulfilled when you accept yourself unconditionally and have a constant experience of positive self-evaluation. It involves knowing your skills and achievements, being aware that you have and will continue to overcome challenges. It means being aware of your talents and potentialities.

When people have confidence in their own abilities they are then able to fulfil more complicated needs that contribute to self-esteem such as cognitive needs. People appear to have a drive for knowledge and personal development. The knowledge may not contribute to the individual's survival but contributes toward a sense of meaning and personal value as knowledge and skills are advanced. Cognitive needs can involve entering into education or watching documentaries on T.V. Perhaps we have a motivation to learn a new language or develop our writing or mathematical skills. Certainly, over the past decade, many older people entered into college courses to develop an understanding of computer skills even though there friends refuse to entertain new-fangled technologies. From infancy our cognitive skills are constantly growing based on need and reward. We have already discussed the importance of social acceptance in a child's development, so their cognitive development will also be affected by social reinforcement. The cognitive needs are more interest based than need based although their will normally be a connective reason behind the choice of learning. This does not necessarily mean that social influence is not active at this stage. Let us not forget that unfulfilled esteem needs will also motivate cognitive development based on the reinforcement of significant others. This could mean that we choose learning based on other peoples preferences and excel at those subjects to receive the flattery and acceptance. This would not lead to self-actualisation as the individual would be motivated by an external locus of evaluation. Some people may attempt to fulfil esteem needs by invalidating other people in order to feel superior. This would perhaps give a temporary feeling of importance but ultimately is an expression of low self-esteem.

Aesthetic expressions are often an expression of an individual's uniqueness and indeed Maslow placed Aesthetic and cognitive needs as an extended model of the Hierarchy between esteem and actualisation. A true sense of self is expressed in the way we arrange our homes, in the music we listen to and the art we appreciate. Many people express these needs in photography, painting and in the clothes they wear. Aesthetic needs will include appreciating the beauty of nature, the sounds of the forest and the peace and relaxation this brings. To have an attractive home or to be in attractive areas is a drive for some people and thy will feel motivated to surround themselves with beauty. Humans have often expressed this need by designing beautiful gardens and just sitting there and enjoying the colours. It is very rare to find someone who feels motivated to sit and relax at a rubbish tip or building site. When we visit an art gallery or listen to some music there is always meaning behind the creativity; something that says something about its creator. Some people would regard such expressions as conceited; but these expressions of self are positive from the point of view that the creator has self-acceptance of their pain and joys and can express this. Some people can be seen not to crave these things because their mind is focused on the lower needs. Esteem is desired very much and some people fish for compliments and praise in many different ways. We can see the individual who struggles to afford fashionable clothing, a big house and an impressive car is maintaining a façade to attract esteem but this will only result in exhaustion as such an individual cannot accept self in any circumstance apart from the illusion they have created.

Fulfilled esteem needs involve valuing yourself and others and being able to accept mistakes as a lessons rather than a dogmatic indicator of worth. Self actualisation can only be reached by the individual who has fulfilled developed self-esteem or unconditional self-acceptance, but what does this mean? And is it realistic?

Actualisation Needs.

Self-Actualisation is rarely reached and is not a fleeting momentary experience but could be compared to a plant that has reached its potential by producing beautiful flowers and fruit. The human potential involves more than activities and deeds but an attitude and perspective of mind that goes beyond programming and instinct. Self Actualised people appear to have their own ability to reason and therefore formulate their own morality based on their genuine experience of empathy which exists independently of any outside influence. In fact a self-actualised individual may reject the morality of their culture and risk death in favour of their own ethical reasoning. Although most Christians would disagree with me it appears to be a fact that Jesus rejected the morality of God as laid down in the Old Testament in favour of 'reasoning and empathy based compassion.' he put forward morality that is more comparable to Buddhism than to anything recognisable in the Torah. On seeing a woman that was about to be stoned to death for adultery he boldly stood there and said to the crowed "He who is without sin may cast the first stone." He was of course killed for this and many other 'blasphemies ', but if you forget about the magical nonsense that is attached to this story, you can see clearly that he was trying to introduce good ethical sense and self-determination. When he said "The truth will make you free," he was probably referring to the self-determination and freedom that comes from being genuine. Certainly we are all free but most of the human race choses to be captive to conditions of worth. The self-actualises individual will be motivated by empathy in their moral perspective rather than being motivated by social or imagined spiritual reward. They are proof that you don't need religion to have morals. This attitude can be seen the wisest people in history. Mohandas Ghandi, The Dalai Lama and Nelson Mandela appear to have this quality. Nietzsche described people with this state of mind as the Overman or sometimes translated Superman, but it refers to an individual who has transcended or gone beyond the programming and instinctual drives to become something more, He refers to the actualising tendency of self-transcendence when he states:

I teach you the Superman. Man is something that is to be surpassed. What have ye done to surpass man? All beings hitherto have created something beyond themselves: and ye want to be the ebb of that great tide, and would rather go back to the beast than surpass man.
Thus Spake Zarathustra : Friedrich Nietzsche 1:3

The idea of going beyond or transcending the self is quite often a goal of those who search for ultimate meaning. It is something that is difficult to reach for as a goal because its nature is outside the normal beliefs regarding the separate nature of self, others and reality. There is a realisation in the individual who is self-actualised that all beings are part of one universe; and although we make our own personal meaning there is the mature and brave realisation of meaninglessness and non-existence. Jean-Paul Sartre States:

We set out upon our pursuit of being, and it seemed to us that the series of our questions had led us to the heart of being. But behold, at the moment when we thought we were arriving at the goal, a glance cast on the question itself has revealed to us suddenly that we are encompassed with nothingness. The permanent possibility of non-being, outside us and within, conditions our questions about being. Furthermore, it is non-being which is going to limit the reply. What being will be must of necessity arise on the basis of what it is not. Whatever being is, it Will allow this formulation: "Being is that and outside of that, nothing."

94

Thus a new component of the real has just appeared to us non-being.
Being and Nothingness: Jean-Paul Sartre, p67.

Such a perspective acknowledges the limits of knowledge and demonstrates that the self-actualised or transcendent individual has outgrown the need to cling to comforting metaphysical fantasies but has rather realised a fundamental reality regarding their relationship to the rest of existence. Sartre refers to non-genuine thoughts and beliefs as bad faith which prevents true transcendence. He continues:

There is then no question of expelling anguish from consciousness nor of constituting it in an unconscious psychic phenomenon; very simply I can make myself guilty of bad faith while apprehending the anguish which I am, and this bad faith, intended to fill up the nothingness which I am in my relation to myself, precisely implies the nothingness which it suppresses.
Being and Nothingness: Jean-Paul Sartre p44

Being able to accept the realities of our existence enables the self actualised individual to experience empathy more deeply than anyone with 'Bad Faith'. Bad faith is a way of hiding from the experience of meaninglessness behind a façade of spiritual fantasy and ego. Rather the self-actualised on realising the reality of nothingness is motivated to bring beaning to the gift of temporary experience by experiencing life with gratitude. The genuine caring for others in the same situation enables the self-actualise to demonstrate unconditional acceptance of people who are suffering. In the I-Ching or Book of Changes the superior Man is mentioned repeatedly as an individual who is a compassionate wise example of leader and teacher. Certainly the self-actualised individual will be compassionate because they have developed a deep empathy based on unconditional acceptance and genuine compassion. There is no ego or false self-image to defend in the self-actualised individual, they are already comfortable and accept themselves unconditionally and offer this same attitude to others. The self-actualised individual is a positive influence in any arena. When working with criminals, delinquent children or the depressed, the self-actualised individual offers their genuine 'self' with all its 'real' qualities. Some would call Self Actualisation a state of realisation, or confuse it with religious experience but anyone who correlates this state as a religious or spiritual experience is missing the point. Self-Actualisation requires an individual to be congruent. This means that they can tolerate ambiguities in the sense that they accept that there are things they cannot know and do not feel the need to attach metaphysical terms such as god or angels to fill those gaps; in fact such spiritual ideas may well reinforce conditions of worth and lower self-esteem. The Self Actualised individual is independent, their need for love and esteem comes from their belief that all people have equal value and that everyone is worthy of respect as a human being. They will not crave a multitude of friends but rather with have just a few very close friends and family with many acquaintances and colleagues that they value. When a self-actualised individual says they will do something, they are true to their word and if they make a decision to take a course of action they will generally see it through.

It is interesting that there is a tendency to equate self actualisation with spiritual experience. The story of the Buddha has been turned into a religion by many but the story of how Siddhartha Gautama had the self-esteem to follow his own path which resulted in social rejection by peers. He them overcame the temptations of the ego until he came to be 'Awake'. Buddha realised that his experiences where a result of his beliefs about reality and his enlightenment required him to become objective regarding those realities. The teachings of the Buddha were not about spirits, gods and worship, but rather about realisation, becoming aware of reality and self. The motivation for Buddha was similar to the motivation of the hierarchy of needs and that motivation was to overcome suffering. In a similar way to Sartre, Buddha concluded that the idea of a self was an illusion and therefore 'ego' is a form of suffering. He put forward that every individual life is a combination of separate parts that make up a whole and therefore the self is temporary and an illusion. The acceptance that life is temporary and precious is a motivating factor in many people's lives. If we are only to live once then we want to get it right and make the most of the time we have, certainly we don't want to waste this chance. The self-actualised individual lives in such a way that they experience life to the full. Perhaps this perspective motivates the compassion self-actualisers are attributed with. Very few people ever find peace in their lives and are plagued by regret or discontent in some way and find comfort in the idea that there is more to life than this existence; however the self-actualised individual realised that although this may be true, there is no evidence to support such an assertion and it is more likely that this life is all there is. This sounds bleak and negative to someone who embraces ideas of 'something else,' but for the self-actualiser the realisation of the temporary nature of life motivates them to love, work and play to the full; and motivates compassion for all those who hide in fear of the reality of life. I have already mentioned some people who could be described as self-actualisers but they are often attached in some people's minds as religious figures; however these people offered teachings and views were based on their own autonomous view points; being motivated by compassion for their fellow human beings rather than advocating a form of religion. In many ways religion is the antithesis of self-actualisation for the reason that spiritual directives requires an individual to suspend compassion and empathy in favour of dogmatic rules that 'must' be obeyed. In most holy books such as the Bible the command to kill or reject those who deviate from the faith is quite prominent. Being moved by compassion has saved more lives than anything else. Self–actualised individuals are rarely known to the world because they are not motivated by 'ego'. In countries where AIDs and malaria killing families we see individuals motivated to bring their scientific medical knowledge to their villages which ease their suffering. We see new medications being developed to cure what appear to be insurmountable illnesses. We see events such as live aid that contributed to easing the suffering of millions. All of these acts of compassion are the mark of a self-actualised individual. Self-actualisation also involves transcendence of needs. We see the expression of self-actualisation in the tendency for the human race to advance. Our knowledge of the stars, gravity and electricity has all come from people who are striving to become all they can be. The human race cannot help but benefit from such individuals. Self-actualisation is seen in so many individual ways. Many people claim to have reached their potential but the truth is that an individual's potential is truly endless. A great musician can also learn to become a great mathematician, actor or engineer. Nature's tendency to actualise cannot be ignored. The universe itself started as an empty space filled with quantum particles that combined to create suns and planets and life. There is no doubt that actualisation is everywhere we look. Self actualisation involves a continuous interaction with life experiencing every moment in the moment. It requires an individual to have a strong sense of self with ethics and the flexibility to change when evidence requires it. People who are self-actualisers are generally non-conformists who start great movements that change society for the better and reinforce human rights and dignity. Freedom and self-determination are the philosophy of the self-actualised individual. Freedom sounds like something that is given to us by state law but the self-actualised individual realised that even in captivity that you are free as long as you do not lose your sense of autonomy.

In psychotherapy and care/support we cannot expect our clients to become self-actualised; it is their own personal goal normally to experience some kind of improvement in their sense of well-being. Assisting individuals to identify and move toward goals can be helpful in stimulating the actualising tendency but we should always allow them to grow as an individual rather than attempting to indoctrinate them with psychological or academic ideologies. If the conditions are correct then the individual will natural grow in their own autonomous direction.

I feel that Rogers explains this attitude perfectly:

It would mean that the therapist feels this client to be a person of unconditional self-worth: of value no matter what his condition, his behaviour, or his feelings. It would mean that the therapist is genuine, hiding behind no defensive façade, but meeting the client with the feelings which organically he is experiencing.
A therapists View Of Psychotherapy: C. Rogers. P185.

Conclusion.

The desire to succeed in care and therapy is strong in any practitioner; however all we can do is offer an environment where growth can take place. We are not a client's entire life and so we cannot offer an entirely perfect environment for them to grow, there are always other influences including their own personal perceptions and conditioning. The only real way we can assist our clients is to maintain our own personal development and make sure that our motives are always based on compassion and empathy rather than ego, introjects or corporate targets. Self-actualisation is a great ideal as a guide but is not a real goal in its self as it would be difficult to measure. The main thing any practitioner can hope to achieve is a constant drive toward awareness. The need to live up to an ideal would be counterproductive to the principles of self-actualisation. There are always people in this world who believe that they have attained enlightenment and lord it over the rest of us as if it were some kind of magic knowledge that they have discovered; but such an attitude would portray low self-esteem. Whether you are self-actualised or not, will not affect your work with clients. The only requirement there is for a practitioner to provide a nurturing environment is to be constantly attentive to personal development through supervision and available courses.

I hope you have found some use for this book. If you have any recommendations or suggestions don't hesitate to email:

Alex@plesseycastle.com

All the best

Alex H Parker

Alex H Parker © 2013

6078498R00058

Printed in Great Britain
by Amazon.co.uk, Ltd.,
Marston Gate.